will leader John Pym live or die? Using an ancient technique called horary, Lilly predicts Pym will die in eight days' time. He is correct.

In the pages of his best-selling pamphlets, Lilly enthralls the civil war-torn nation with his uncannily accurate forecasts of who will triumph in combat. Parliament's new prophet directly influences the course of war by advising the New Model Army when to fight, based on his judgement of Charles I's horoscope – the key Battle of Naseby is won with this insight.

Lauded as England's Merlin, Parliament sends him to the battlefield to boost morale with astral propaganda. At the same time, mercurial and wily Lilly provides stellar counsel to both the King and the rising radical sects. His status as the nation's arch magus is sealed when he correctly foresees Charles's death.

Now the most famous man in England's republic and the leader of a growing counter-culture group, Lilly's extraordinary influence is revealed when his warning words about a solar eclipse scare the country to a standstill. But not everyone is happy about his visions of the future and their effect on public order: ministers try to outlaw the star science and he is charged with sedition.

Worse is to come in the Restoration world. In private, Charles II and the elite still seek Lilly's guidance, but in public the Establishment moves to silence him and ban prophecy. In 1666, when his forecast of a great fire engulfing London comes true, he is suspected of starting the blaze. Can his astonishing gift help him best those in power, and save his profession and his life?

'Catherine Blackledge's biography is not just required reading for every would-be astrologer. It stands alone as an amazing tale full of insight into pivotal history. *The Man Who Saw The Future* is fascinating and wonderfully well written.' **Jonathan Cainer, astrologer and broadcaster**

'William Lilly was an astrologer, magician and free-thinker with connections that went to the heart of republican and Restoration England. Catherine Blackledge's excellent new biography tells the story of a man whose life and deeds are essential for an understanding of England on the boundary of the medieval and modern worlds.' **Dr Nicholas Campion, University of Wales Trinity Saint David**

'Advisor; confidant; propagandist; hotline to the voice of God: opinions differed, but astrologer William Lilly could not be ignored. In this vivid depiction of his life and practice, Catherine Blackledge brings from the shadows one of the period's major players at a turning-point in our history.' **John Frawley, author of** *The Real Astrology*

'An elegant, informed and highly readable exposition of a confusing, almost forbidden chapter of UK history. Astrologers and history fans alike will be fascinated.' **Neil Spencer, writer and astrologer, author of** *True As the Stars Above*

'A very exciting and colourful read, which offers a unique view of the dramatic events of Stuart England through the eyes of an astrologer – and makes a plea for the enduring value of astrology on the way.' **Professor Ronald Hutton, University of Bristol, author of** *Pagan Britain*

'A book that brings the extraordinary astrologer William Lilly and his times vividly to life. It is essential reading for anyone studying Lilly and the astrology of the 17th-century in England.' **Vernon Wells, Company of Astrologers**

A Biography of WILLIAM LILLY

THE MAN WHO SAW THE FUTURE

The 17th-Century Astrologer who Changed
the Course of the English Civil War

CATHERINE BLACKLEDGE

Foreword by Professor Owen Davies

WATKINS

Sharing Wisdom Since
1893

This edition first published in the UK and USA 2015 by
Watkins, an imprint of Watkins Media Limited
19 Cecil Court
London WC2N 4HE

enquiries@watkinspublishing.co.uk

Design and typography copyright © Watkins Media Limited, 2015
Text copyright © Catherine Blackledge 2015

1 3 5 7 9 10 8 6 4 2

Designed and typeset by Manisha Patel
Project editor: Rebecca Sheppard
Managing editor: Deborah Hercun

Printed and bound in Europe

A CIP record for this book is available from the British Library

ISBN: 978-1-78028-800-0

The abbreviations CE and BCE are used in this book:
CE Common Era (the equivalent of AD)
BCE Before the Common Era (the equivalent of BC)

www.watkinspublishing.com

'All things are known to the astrologer. All that has taken place in the past, all that will happen in the future – everything is revealed to him, since he knows the effects of the heavenly motions which have been, those which are, and those which will be, and since he knows at what time they will act, and what effects they ought to produce.'

Guido Bonatti, *Decem Tractatus Astronomiae*

To the student in astrology
'My friend, whoever thou art, that with so much ease shalt receive the benefit of my hard studies, and doest intend to proceed in this heavenly knowledge of the stars ... As thou daily conversest with the heavens ... be humane, courteous, familiar to all ... be not dismayed, if ill spoken of ...'

William Lilly, *Christian Astrology*

'I'm telling you stories. Trust me.'

Jeanette Winterson, *The Passion*

For Steve and Willow Rose

Acknowledgments

This book exists because Elias Ashmole preserved William Lilly's casebooks, notes, letters and almanacs. I am grateful to the Bodleian Library, Oxford, and the British Library, London, for granting me access to these documents.

The work would not have been possible either without an appreciation of the 17th-century astrological techniques and sidereal theory used by William Lilly and his peers. My gratitude goes to all those who have helped me become a student of astrology. My greatest debt in this regard is to Lilly and his glorious, magisterial *Christian Astrology*.

Many people – astrologers, historians, friends and family – have shared their research and insight, read drafts of the manuscript in its various stages of incarnation, or simply provided much-needed support and encouragement. Thanks go to: Vernon Wells, Jennifer Trueland, Graeme Tobyn, Neil Spencer, Lynn Rawlinson, Ronald Hutton, Michael Hunter, Deborah Houlding, John Frawley, Dee Dawson, Owen Davies, Patrick Curry, Geoffrey Cornelius, Bernard Capp, Nicolas Campion, Jonathan Cainer and, in particular, Michael Mann at Watkins.

Most importantly, my thanks and love go to Steve and Willow; you two form my lodestone in this beautiful, mysterious world.

Contents

Foreword

by Professor Owen Davies

The story of William Lilly's life is a glinting mirror of his times, the man himself no mere observer but inextricably woven into the rich narrative of the political and religious history of mid 17th-century England. During the Civil War years he walked the tightrope between royalist and parliamentarian patronage, his criticism of the monarchy encoded in his astrological prophecies. Come the Restoration and Lilly was selling tens of thousands of his almanac a year. Since he was a conspicuous London figure, it is no surprise to find Samuel Pepys recording in his diary for October 1660 an evening spent in Lilly's study, singing and chewing over astrological matters. His fame was enhanced further by his apparent prediction of the Great Fire of London in 1666.

So, Lilly is hardly a forgotten figure. He has been the subject of a couple of books, and is acknowledged as a key figure of his age in histories of English astrology, but I have long thought that there was space for a new biography of this extraordinary man, one that took into account recent studies in the field, and explored something of his 'inner life'. My mind turned to doing this a couple of years ago, but as if governed by some obscure astrological conjunction, Dr Catherine Blackledge contacted me out of the blue to say that she was well advanced in doing this very task. It has been my pleasure to read the resulting book.

While he was both celebrated and derided as an astrologer, Lilly's private interests in the occult, and by this I mean the hidden and secret power of the natural world, were much wider than natural and judicial astrology. Lilly and his fraternity went on treasure-hunting expeditions using his dowsing sticks, or 'Mosaical Rods' as they were grandly called. He attempted to communicate with the Queen of the Fairies, and he created sigils (magical symbols) and charms for protection. Like his fellow male and female astrologers of the era, Lilly was as much a physician as a prognosticator. He was a 'piss-prophet' who inspected his clients' urine to detect what ailed them – perhaps the pox or possibly witchcraft (his casebooks reveal numerous instances of bewitched clients). The planets that governed different healing plants and dictated the most astrologically propitious moments to harvest them were crucial ingredients in popular herbals of the period, most notably those written by Lilly's acquaintance Nicholas Culpeper.

Blackledge's history of Lilly does much more than provide an account of the man himself: it depicts an intellectual world on the cusp of change. While Lilly and his fellow members of the Society of Astrologers pondered over their celestial calculations, a profound debate was taking place as to the nature of the world and the heavens, a debate that was central to the future of science and religion. On one side there were those who upheld the reality of a material realm imbued with myriad intangible spiritual forces – a conception of God's creation that allowed for the existence of witches, demons, ghosts and miracles. On the other side were those, inspired by the likes of Descartes, who proposed that matter was a passive substance, and who saw the heavens as a distant, mechanistic, mathematical realm. There were many who situated themselves in various stages between the two extremes. Astrology was caught in the middle. For some, it was a science that had a clock-like philosophy of causation based on the ancient notion that the radiating essence of the planets and stars influenced every aspect of the mundane world. But others held a more mystical perspective best summed up in the hermetic philosophy, 'As above, so below', which saw the universe as connected and ensouled. These debates, though, were of little interest to, or beyond the understanding of, many of Lilly's considerable clientele, which ranged from the aristocracy and Members of Parliament to servant girls. In a chaotic world, astrology, and the magical and medical services it facilitated, provided a sense of order and succour.

Thanks to his popular publications, Lilly's name was one to be conjured with across the land. Cunning-folk from Essex to Somerset impressed their clients with their boasts of having learned their occult knowledge from the London oracle. His influence on popular culture stretched long beyond his lifetime. Original editions of *Christian Astrology*, his three-volume guide to the sidereal science, were much-sought items in the second-hand occult book trade of the 19th century. These volumes were to be found on the bookshelves of rural and urban cunning-folk and astrologers, alongside the works of more recent rising stars in the almanac business, such as Raphael and Zadkiel. Lilly's influence continued to permeate popular belief and practice through his later readership, just as Culpeper's proved an enduring influence on 19th-century popular medicine.

Blackledge's story of Lilly's life and times, based in part on his own posthumously published autobiography, and drawing upon original archive material as well as academic studies, illuminates the enduring reach of this charismatic character and his application of astrology for the masses. By taking an imaginative and sometimes speculative approach to her subject, one that academics usually fear adopting, we gain fresh insight into a tumultuous period, and are drawn closer to the man and his interpretation of the world around him – one that is far from dead.

Introduction

At exactly 11am on Monday 15 September 2003, a commemorative plaque was unveiled in the heart of London in honour of one of England's unsung luminaries – the 17th-century astrologer William Lilly (1602–1681).

To be eligible for what are known as 'Westminster plaques', individuals must be highly regarded by their profession, have made a positive contribution to human welfare or happiness and be either recognizable to the well-informed passer-by or deserving of national recognition. The first person to be celebrated in this way was Sir Winston Churchill; others include Oscar Wilde and computer pioneer Charles Babbage. Lilly was the 53rd recipient of a plaque, and the first astrologer.

What is it about Lilly? Coming from a humble farming family, he rose by his own efforts to become the most famous man in England – more acclaimed than Charles I or Oliver Cromwell. He was a publishing sensation and the nation's first ever media darling (celebrated in print and song), thanks to his bestselling pamphlets containing uncannily accurate forecasts about events of national importance.

During the Civil War, he was a key figure consulted at the highest level by the King and Parliament, as well as by the radical sects. His astrological intelligence on the timing of critical battles helped win the war for Parliament. A true democrat, he was committed to making the science of the stars accessible to all, whatever their background. He helped everyone who came to him, even those who could not pay.

Because of Lilly, astrology became a mass phenomenon; he held the populace in thrall with his predictions and had the power to bring the nation to a standstill. But the hold he had over the public concerned and angered establishment figures, and many tried to silence him. William outwitted his opponents again and again.

Universities study his writings, associations still celebrate his life; his entry in the Dictionary of National Biography of necessity runs to several pages. He was talented, charming, mercurial, democratic and wily, but it is only in recent years that the full extent of his influence and vision has begun to be appreciated. As the city of London identified, William Lilly is deserving of national recognition.

Chapter 1

The Piss-prophet Rises

The Sun signifies the self, kingship and confidence,
the father, the masculine principle and the hero.
It is associated with gold, sunflowers, the lion and the eagle,
rubies, royal courts and palaces, and the heart.

William Lilly considered the flask of urine held out to him. In the light from the lanthorn hanging above the entrance to the Corner House, the thin, swirling liquid gleamed golden-yellow; the face behind it was in shadow. It was early evening in London on the last day of November 1643 and he had been ready to finish work. But here was another case to judge. Taking the vial, he beckoned the stranger on the doorstep, then turned to note the time from the iron chamber clock on the wall. It was five hours and 53 minutes after noon.

Settling his new client, Lilly placed the flask of urine on a sturdy oak table and opened up his casebook again. The pages showed it had been another busy day for the rising 41-year-old astrologer. He had greeted his first customer, a maid from Kent, at 7.20am; she was keen to know whether to say yes or no to a marriage proposal. He counselled her not to marry the 'proud young fellow' she was in love with. A better match lay in the future, if she could wait.

Her query 'Should I marry?' was one of the most common Lilly heard. But it was the more general 'What is to be done?' that was the most popular question asked at the Corner House, his home situated at the eastern end of the Strand – a stone's throw from the north bank of the Thames and a brisk ten-minute walk from either the burgeoning City to the east, or from Whitehall and Westminster to the west.

No two days were the same. Any problem might be brought to him, and he typically answered a fascinating assortment of questions. His second client on this particular day had wanted to know whether he was bewitched or not, and if not, what ailed him? The next lady was a returning customer: satisfied with Lilly's services last time, she had come back because she was curious about the cause of her husband's anger.

Later, he had been challenged to find the culprit who had stolen a tankard from the Sun Inn in Westminster – he identified two men. Mid-afternoon, Mr Fowler enquired if it would be good for him to join a shipping voyage to the East Indies. His last two clients, both ladies, were struggling with situations wrought by the Civil War. The first asked, 'Is my husband alive?' The second, 'When will my son be home?'

His clientele's background revealed astrology's social reach: around 20 per cent of his customers were of noble birth; another 20 per cent worked in traditional trades and crafts; 15 per cent were seafarers; less than one per cent were paupers; military men and professionals, such as lawyers and physicians, each represented five per cent; with female servants making up the rest – and the majority – of his client list.

The Civil War was changing Lilly's caseload. Since Charles I, King of England, had raised his standard against the forces on the side of Parliament in August 1642, people burdened with a different set of concerns had been arriving at his door. In a time of limited and slow correspondence, the distressed and the scared sought clarity about the whereabouts and wellbeing of family; many wondered if their offspring should go to war or which side they should support; one customer had simply asked: 'Whether good to adhere to King or country?'

Gaining military insight was a common aim. Would the King's nephew Prince Rupert gain honour by the wars, and would he worst Parliament's general, the Earl of Essex? Would Charles I procure help from Irish forces? Was the report that Cambridge had been taken by the King's army true? Would the Earl of Essex take the town of Reading? These questions had all been posed recently.

A matter of national importance and a recommendation from a satisfied customer had brought the client in front of him now. The testimonial had come from Bulstrode Whitelocke, a lawyer and influential parliamentarian who, during the build-up to war, was one of the Members of Parliament involved in wresting power from the King. Whitelocke had recently become Lilly's friend and champion after experiencing the star-gazer's extraordinary skills: the MP had fallen ill a few months earlier and, aware of Lilly's reputation, he had sent a friend to the Corner House with a sample of his urine.

Lilly judged that Whitelocke would initially recover, but he warned that within one month he would suffer a dangerous relapse brought on by overindulgence. Whitelocke recovered quickly, as predicted, but ignored the rest of Lilly's counsel and before the month was out he fell violently ill after eating too much trout. With his physician despairing whether he would live, a frightened Whitelocke turned to Lilly again.

The astrologer's prognosis – that the MP was not facing death and would be well within five to six weeks – once more proved true. Whitelocke showed his gratitude by introducing the astrologer to his circle of parliamentary colleagues, among them Sir Philip Stapleton,

Robert Reynolds and Denzil Holles. Lilly's association with Parliament had begun.

The pot of urine brought to the Corner House that evening symbolized the growing regard many parliamentarians now had for Lilly. Its contents belonged to John Pym, the leader of Parliament and the most influential man in the country after the King.

Since November 1640, when Charles I had called Parliament to meet for the first time after eleven years of personal rule, it was the vocal and articulate Pym who had led opposition to the monarch in the House of Commons. It was Pym who drew up the Grand Remonstrance, a provocative document listing Charles's misdeeds against the country and demanding religious and political reform, which was passed by Parliament at the end of November 1641. Pym was then one of the five MPs whom an incensed Charles tried and failed to arrest for treason six weeks later.

When war became a reality, it was Pym who was the architect of Parliament's forces: he raised the funds to finance the army by creating a new system of taxation and organized the network of parliamentary committees governing during wartime. When, in mid-1643, military fortune favoured the King's men, it was Pym who negotiated and concluded an important alliance with Scottish Covenanters in the late autumn. Strengthened in numbers and spirit, Parliament's reinvigorated forces now had a chance to seize control of the fighting.

But suddenly Pym was worryingly ill: too ill to leave his sickbed. The gentleman at the Corner House was a concerned friend sent by an alarmed Parliament; Pym was not aware his urine was being brought for astrological analysis, the visitor told Lilly, but could he help – would he look into the future and tell him whether John Pym would live or die? Nodding his assent, Lilly got to work.

The craft he was practising was an ancient one. Correlating the movement of the planets and stars above with events on Earth below had provided a way of understanding the universe since the people of Mesopotamia had first begun observing and recording 'the writing of heaven' in the 3rd millennium BCE. The science of the stars was the first great theory of everything.

At its heart was judging the nature of time: is this a good moment to set out on a journey?; does this point in life support entering into marriage?; if we fight now, will we win? Four main branches of what was known as judicial astrology (astrology that made a judgement) developed over the centuries, each with its own set of complex sidereal rules. Mundane or world astrology was concerned with the rise and fall of royalty, dynasties and nations; natal or genethlialogical astrology looked at the lives of individuals; elections focused on selecting auspicious moments; while horary (or interrogations) was the art of answering any question depending on the time it was delivered.

Lilly was going to use horary astrology (the name means 'of the hour') to divine Pym's prospects. It was the most common astrological technique of the era because, in the hands of a skilled astromancer, it provided clear-cut and detailed answers quickly on any topic, and without the need for an accurate time and place of birth (which many people did not possess).

All that was needed for a horary was the time and location the question was posited, or, if it was a medical problem, when the urine was presented. For health queries, it was the precise moment the sample was received that had the greatest significance (rather than any physical facts about the fluid); this was why men like Lilly were called 'piss-prophets'.

Using his ephemeris (a reference booklet containing tables of planetary positions), and knowing the latitude of his work place in London, 51°, Lilly calculated the position in the zodiac (the invisible path around the Earth along which the Sun, Moon and planets appear to move) of each of the seven classical planets – Sun ☉, Moon ☽, Mercury ☿, Venus ♀, Mars ♂, Jupiter ♃ and Saturn ♄. He also looked at which sign of the zodiac (which of the twelve equal sections of the zodiac) each planet was in – it could be Aries ♈, Taurus ♉, Gemini ♊, Cancer ♋, Leo ♌, Virgo ♍, Libra ♎, Scorpio ♏, Sagittarius ♐, Capricorn ♑, Aquarius ♒ or Pisces ♓. After, he calculated the astrologically significant points known as the Part of Fortune ⊗ and the North Node ☊ or Dragon's Head.

With this information, he could then begin to draw up the figure of heaven (astrological chart) for the moment he had received Pym's urine. In the 17th century, this two-dimensional representation of the position of the planets was depicted in a square setting (PLATE 1, FACING PAGE, TOP, shows Lilly's chart). Modern astrological charts are typically circular (CHART 1, FACING PAGE, BOTTOM).

Charts are also subdivided into twelve sections, known as the houses of heaven, and Lilly had to calculate which house each planet occupied (in his square chart the twelve houses are depicted by the triangles around the inner square; in the modern version by truncated slices of a pie). Each house signifies a particular facet of human life – the second denotes money, the third siblings, the fifth children, the eighth death and the twelfth secret enemies. The first house begins at the middle left of the chart (at a point known as the Ascendant); subsequent houses follow in a counter-clockwise order.

It took Lilly about ten minutes to cast the chart. Now he had to judge it using horary's specific rules. In the ancient star science's language, the planet ruling the zodiac sign at the start (or cusp) of the first house symbolized Pym. In his horary chart, the sign was Cancer, which meant that the Moon (Cancer's planetary ruler) was his signifier. The position of the Moon confirmed Pym's poor state of health straightaway: it was within five degrees of the sixth house, the house of illness.

PLATE 1 Will John Pym live or die? 30 November 1643
(reproduced with permission of the Bodleian Libraries, The University of Oxford, Ashm.548(3), p.130)

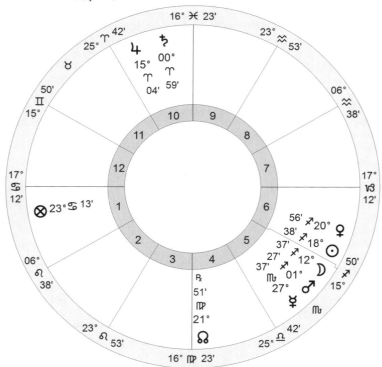

CHART 1 Will John Pym live or die? 30 November 1643

Knowledge of the nature of the parliamentary leader's ailment was drawn from the zodiac sign the Moon ruled – Cancer. In astral theory, each sign signified a particular area of the body: Aries ruled the head, Taurus the neck, Gemini the arms and hands, Cancer the breasts and belly, through to Capricorn ruling the knees, Aquarius the ankles, and Pisces the feet.

Lilly then analysed whether the Moon was in any angular relationships (or aspects) with other planets in the chart. There were five possibilities: planets could be in opposition to each other (180° distant from one another), trine (120° distant), sextile (30°), quartile or square (90°), and conjuct or in conjunction with each other (when the planets were adjacent).

Overall, the information led him to pinpoint Pym's stomach as the source of the sickness. Ruling out poisoning, he diagnosed digestive problems caused by a stoppage of some kind in the belly. The next step was the prognosis. For this, he looked at the Moon's movements in recent days and through into the future: with which planets in the chart had the fast-moving Moon come into contact with, or was going to? When would such meetings take place? The portents were ominous.

The day before, the Moon had conjoined in the heavens with the malevolent planet Mars and the malefic fixed star *Cor Scorpii* (the Scorpion's Heart or Antares), which was associated with sickness and death. In addition, the Moon was, in the words of the mantic art, combust (moving to conjunction) with the Sun in the house of disease – this signified death.

The last question was when death would occur. Lilly's forecast was that the parliamentary leader would die in eight days' time. He assessed this by looking at the Moon's movements, and at the planet ruling the zodiac sign at the start of the house of death (the eighth house). In Pym's chart, this sign was Aquarius, which is ruled by Saturn.

By William's calculations, the length of time left to live came from the number of days it took the Moon to move from its current position in the zodiac sign of Sagittarius to one where it was adjacent to Saturn. Checking in his ephemeris, Lilly noted that the Moon and Saturn would meet on Friday 8 December. This, he told Pym's friend, was when the great man would die.

Closing the door after his guest had departed, Lilly paused briefly to take in the weight of the verdict he had just given. Pym's death would be a great shock to the parliamentary cause and would leave a gaping hole in its leadership. How would Parliament's men react, and how would the King respond?

At this point, it was hard to say which side – King or Parliament – William was wholly for. Such a stance was not unusual. At this time very few were against monarchy altogether: Parliament insisted it was fighting 'for King and Parliament', and MPs hoped genuinely for a negotiated settlement.

William helped anybody who came to him, whatever their allegiance. He had chosen to continue to live and work in the parliamentary stronghold of London and was increasingly well-known and respected within parliamentary circles.

Yet he had cavalier leanings too: he believed in and approved of monarchy and enjoyed the friendship of those who supported the King. One of his closest friends was the royalist Sir William Pennington of Muncaster in the county of Cumberland and today, having done all he could to support Parliament, Lilly was about to head out to help Pennington.

Lilly and Pennington had met in 1634, shortly after Lilly had begun practising astrology and not long after he had wed for a second time. However, married life had not been running smoothly, and instead of being at home with his new bride, William had chosen to embark on a gentlemen's night out. The occasion was a treasure-hunting expedition organized by their mutual friend, the King's clockmaker, Davy Ramsey (finding hidden treasure was something of a craze in the 16th and 17th centuries).

Ramsey, who dabbled in the occult, had heard there was a great quantity of treasure buried in the cloisters of Westminster Abbey. Eager to find out if this was true, he sought permission to hunt from John Williams, the Bishop of Lincoln. Yes, they could go ahead, the bishop said, with the proviso that if any treasure was discovered, his church should have a share of it. So, late one winter's night, equipped with a 'half quartern sack' to put the treasure in, Ramsey, Lilly, Pennington and more than twenty other gentlemen and their aides entered the Abbey.

Lilly was known for his knowledge of the dark arts, as well as astrology, and it was he and an acquaintance, John Scott of Pudding Lane, who led the search using mosaical or divining rods (hazel rods used to locate metal or water). As William later recalled, the two men 'played the hazel-rods round about the cloister'. What they were waiting for was the rods to turn one over another – this would be 'an argument that the treasure was there'.

Then it happened: 'upon the west-side of the cloisters' the rods moved together and crossed. It was time to dig. Standing back, the gentlemen watched with rising anticipation as their men wielded spades and pickaxes. Eventually, after digging 'at least six foot deep' into the floor of the Abbey, they unearthed a coffin, but after deliberating, the party decided not to open it, which they afterwards 'much repented'.

But then, as the disappointed group was walking back from the cloisters into the Abbey church, the unexpected occurred. All of a sudden, a wind rose up, 'so fierce, so high, so blustering and loud' that the men 'verily believed the west-end of the church would have fallen upon us; our rods would not move at all; the candles and torches, all but one, were extinguished, or burned very dimly.'

In the dark, with a strange gale howling around them, the terrified gents looked to Lilly and John Scott. After a pale and amazed-looking Scott admitted he 'knew not what to think or do', William took control. Being well versed in magical practices, including how to communicate with spirits; he stood firm and delivered the correct directions for the dismissal of daemons set to guard treasure. His commands finished, 'all was quiet again,' and each man 'returned into his lodging late, about 12 a-clock at night'.

It had not been a successful treasure-hunting night: Lilly blamed the daemons' anger and the consequent failure to find anything on the presence of too many people, and the laughter and derision from some in the party. Despite this, lasting friendships had been made. Pennington and Lilly became comrades in arms, with William describing Pennington as an 'ever bountiful friend' and his 'most munificent patron'.

Now, on this cold November evening nearly ten years later, Lilly's last task of the day was to help Pennington avoid having his goods and lands seized as part of the campaign to sequestrate royalist estates that Parliament had begun earlier in the year. Pennington was under threat of sequestration because in 1642 Charles I made him one of his commissioners of array and, as such, he had put his signature to an array warrant for raising royalist troops. It was this one document identifying him as on the King's side that was now coming back to haunt him.

A few days ago, Lilly had discovered that John Musgrave, the man who had the array warrant confirming Pennington as a royalist and who was threatening him with sequestration, was in London. Making his acquaintance, Lilly had pretended to be one of Pennington's bitter enemies. Musgrave was charmed by Lilly and, delighted to meet someone who apparently shared his feelings and who could perhaps help him snare his man, he had agreed to join him for a drink.

Now, greeting Musgrave at their arranged meeting place, the Five Bells Inn, Lilly soon realized that luck was on his side. It was almost too easy. Musgrave was eager to show him the array warrant: he asked if Lilly could confirm it was signed in Pennington's hand. Hearing it was, he laid the warrant, together with other documents, down on their table – all William had to do now was to find an opportunity to remove it from him.

Thinking quickly, Lilly looked around for a way to distract the other man. Letting their candle burn out, he passed it over to Musgrave, who was closer to the inn's fire, and asked him to re-light it. Turning away, Musgrave left the table briefly, and William made his move, grabbing the warrant and slipping it into his boots. Minutes later, feigning tiredness, he concluded their business and left for home. His day's work was finally done.

His subterfuge was a resounding success: Musgrave did not even miss the document until a week later, by which time it was in the post to Pennington, with a friendly caveat from William attached – 'sin no more'.

* * *

A dispirited, mournful mood pervaded the House of Commons. Only a few weeks had passed since John Pym's ceremonial burial in Westminster Abbey. Pym had died on 8 December 1643, eight days after his urine had been taken to William Lilly. On dissection, Pym's physicians had found a fist-sized growth in his belly, large enough to be felt from the outside, which had been interfering with his digestion (the tumour may have been cancerous).

Lilly's piss-prophecy had pinpointed precisely the nature and timing of the parliamentary leader's illness and death – and now Parliament's piss-prophet was about to reveal his potential as its spin-doctor too.

In the House, a low murmur of rustling, turning pages and the occasional comment passing to and fro broke the sombre silence. At this point, just a handful of members were reading the pamphlet: Bulstrode Whitelocke was the first (he had been given a manuscript copy by Lilly).

The Speaker of the House spotted him; then Whitelocke's cronies got hold of copies. Then with news spreading quickly about this rousing, must-read booklet, more and more MPs joined them and the noise grew steadily louder, until the House was in a ferment of raised, agitated voices.

Merlinus Anglicus Junior ('England's Little Merlin'), Lilly's first almanac, was the source of the commotion. Almanacs were pocket-sized pamphlets containing astrological forecasts for the year ahead. Often incorporating a calendar and useful information on farming, fairs and physic, they were essential reference books – the original personal organizers. Popular and cheap (typically a penny or tuppence), they were also the country's most favoured reading material: in a nation of between four to five million they were read by one in three households. Even the devil, it was said, possessed a current copy.

Depending on the author, almanacs incorporated gossip, health advice, tips on when it was best to enjoy sex, how much sleep to have to avoid being the 'most drowsy drumbledozy', and even comments on fashion: for example, when lap dogs were *de rigueur* at the start of the 17th century, Edward Pond dismissed them as 'effeminate follies'. They were the first lifestyle magazines, with a broad appeal, as summed up by astrologer Richard Allestree in 1622:

> Wit, learning, order, elegance of phrase,
> health, and the art to lengthen out our days,

Philosophy, physic and poesie,
All this, and more, is in this book to see.

Politically and prophetically speaking, though, almanacs tended to be staid affairs – devoid of controversial predictions and reverential in tone to regal and religious leaders. 'Curse not the King, no not in thy thoughts, and curse not the rich in thy bedchamber' was a typical admonition in their pages. The lack of astrological vigour was due to the fact that, until very recently, the prognostic content of English almanacs was controlled tightly by stringent press censorship.

Such close monitoring of astrologers and their forecasts was not unusual. For centuries, the world's ruling elite had recognized that prophecies could wreak havoc, and that a leader's birth chart, in particular, possessed considerable political value because it could be used to predict the individual's life span. Hence, restrictions on how astrologers practised and promulgated their art were long-standing and widespread.

The first emperor of Rome, Augustus (63 BCE–14 CE), had issued a decree banning astrologers from making death predictions and offering private consultations. His successor Tiberius, on hearing of a plot against the imperial family supported by astrological advice, executed those involved and had Rome's other star-gazers expelled from the city. The frequent expulsion orders from Rome and Roman Italy during the time of the emperors, when the celestial art was not under state control, were typically connected to situations of political instability.

However, for the vast majority of its history, astrology was the preserve of the elite in society: astrologers lived and worked as political and medical advisers at court, where they depended on their sovereign's patronage for survival. Consequently, in the Western world, the problem of having to police astrological promulgations became acute only during the 15th century when two key developments happened

– astrologers began to practise outside the immediate court circle, and the invention of the printing press enabled the mass production and widespread distribution of astrological literature.

From then on, leaders across Europe were forced to employ various means to control almanacs, as well as their authors. Early methods were direct and personal. In Italy in 1474, two University of Bologna astrologers forecast the fifth Duke of Milan's impending demise. Outraged and concerned about the effect on public order, Duke Galeazzo Maria Sforza threatened to cut the star-gazers into pieces (*tagliare a pezi!*) if they did not desist from publishing the death prophecy and forced them to circulate a more palatable, albeit falsified, prediction. (The meddling duke did not escape his fate and was murdered two years later.)

Events in continental Europe in 1524 showed how hard it was to control printed prophecy. Mass panic erupted that year after numerous almanacs forecast a deluge of biblical proportions as a consequence of all seven planets meeting in the water sign of Pisces in February. People built arks, and many fled to high ground or sought sanctuary in penitential rites and processions. With the impending horrors broadcast in ballads and print, this was the world's first media event.

More recently in Italy, Pope Urban VIII had written a papal bull against anyone broadcasting predictions about the death of princes or popes: to do so was now a treasonable offence. Urban was a proficient astrologer himself. He could cast a chart and predict someone's life span – a skill he used to ascertain when cardinals resident in Rome would die; and he made sure his papal election occurred at an auspicious moment.

He even released the occult philosopher and heretic Tommaso Campanella from jail in order that Campanella could design an astrological safe room at the papal palace of Castel Gandolfo.

Decorated with specific stones, plants and colours to counteract malign rays from heaven and pull down benefic ones, this was where Urban decamped to during solar and lunar eclipses.

His papal bull of May 1630 was triggered when a covert astrological political think-tank based at a monastery in Rome announced forecasts of Urban's imminent death across Europe. Its writings were so successful that cardinals from as far afield as Spain and Germany set off for the Vatican, keen to be present for the calling of the conclave to elect a new pontiff. Urban's retaliation included dismantling the astrological intelligence house and imprisoning its leader, Abbott Orazio Morandi. The abbot died in mysterious circumstances in prison before his case could come to trial.

In England, regulations to control astrologers and the content of almanacs had been in place since the 15th century. Laws against prophecy were first enacted in 1402 and 1406; Henry VII then declared that prophecy based on 'arms, fields, names, cognizances or badges' was banned (a coat of arms was interpreted in much the same way as an astrological chart).

Elizabeth I confirmed this latter act and extended legislation. From her reign onwards, forecasting a monarch's demise was forbidden. This ruling was then widened in 1581 to make casting the ruler's birth chart (also known as a nativity or geniture) an act of treason.

From 1603 (when James I became King of England), regulation of almanacs was tightened. James granted a monopoly to carry out censorship to the Company of Stationers (working with the ecclesiastical authorities).

The Company of Stationers' restrictions specified: 'All conjurors and framers of almanacs and prophecies exceeding the limits of allowable astrology shall be punished severely in their person. And we forbid all printers and booksellers, under the same penalties, to print or expose for sale, any almanacs or prophecies which shall not first have been seen and revised by the archbishop, the bishop (or those who shall be expressly appointed for that purpose), and approved of by their certificates, and, in addition, shall have permission from us or from our ordinary judges.'

The resulting Crown control of printing was highly effective. During the 1630s, only one almanac author, John Booker, risked prosecution by including political speculation in his publications. In 1632, Booker commented on corruption in government and the law. In the following year, as the then Bishop William Laud pushed authoritarian religious policies, he had the temerity to prophesy 'wonderful change in the church'; further offensive remarks in his 1634 publication resulted in his being imprisoned.

But in 1641, as Parliament strove to wrest power from the King, the stringent censorship system collapsed: the result was print pandemonium. As well as increased numbers of almanacs and religious tracts, news pamphlets appeared, as did play-pamphlets containing politico-sexual satire, and later in the year the first newsbook (the forerunner of today's newspaper).

London, with its 80 per cent male literacy rate, was now a heady swirl of ink as the records of city bookseller George Thomason reveal. In 1640, Thomason bought 24 publications; in 1641 this rose to 721; and in 1642 he purchased 2,134.

'Buy a new almanac,' chapmen called as they hawked their penny pamphlets. 'What news?' was one of the most frequently used greetings, while on the cobblestones outside St Paul's Cathedral, where the public clustered to purchase the latest booklet, mercury men and women sang out:

> Come buy my new almanacs every one,
> Come pick over your choice before they be gone;

One thousand six hundred fifty and one,
Come buy my new almanacs buy.

In a bid to curb the rapid proliferation of inflammatory tracts, Parliament had introduced limited press licensing in 1643, but it was too little too late. Print as a means of mass communication was now firmly entrenched as part of popular culture. More worryingly for those currently holding positions of authority, the medium of print was also increasingly the technique by which support for alternative and radical causes was being mobilized.

England's Civil War was far from being just a battle between the King and his people: it was also a time of fundamentally rethinking who held authority. The royal right to rule and traditional ecclesiastical command were under threat, but in this new political landscape, where did the source of authority lie? Who could be trusted to interpret scripture and God's signs in the world?

The moment at which Lilly began his prophetical print career was a highly unusual and unique one. A power vacuum was opening up and creative, articulate individuals were taking advantage of it, especially in print. With the publication of *Merlinus Anglicus Junior*, William seized this unprecedented opportunity.

Right from the start, readers of his *Anglicus* were in no doubt about the source of its authority. God's will, Lilly reminded them, was written in the heavens in the rhythmic dance of the planets, and it was the starry language of astrology that was the key to deciphering these celestial plans. 'God rules all by divine providence, and the stars by his permission are instruments whereby many contingent [unknown] events may be foreseen ...' The stars, he explained, give 'some small glimpses of the great affairs God intends upon earth'.

Emphasizing that the planets' motions revealed God's design for the world strengthened the potential influence of Lilly's words immeasurably. It also highlighted astrology's propaganda potential. As the MPs in the Commons quickly realized, what greater rallying cry could there be than to be certain that yours was the cause that was celestially sanctioned? That is why they were looking so eagerly at Lilly's view of what the heavens foretold.

To predict what the year ahead would bring for the English nation, Lilly cast a chart for the start of 1644 (CHART 2, BELOW), which in the 17th century began at the spring equinox when the Sun made its entry or ingress into the zodiac sign of Aries. It was important to him that his audience follow his astrological reasoning, so his

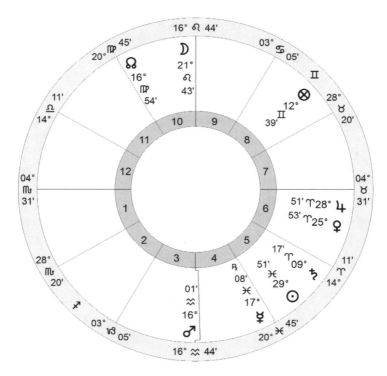

CHART 2 England's ingress chart for 1644 (based on Lilly's original chart for Saturday 9 March at 9.25pm)

pamphlet also included a reference horoscopic chart detailing the meaning of each of the twelve astrological houses, and highlighting, in particular, how readers could differentiate between the fortunes of the King and Parliament.

'When I speak of the tenth house, I intend somewhat of Kings,' he wrote, 'When mention is made of the first house … I intend the Commonalty in general.' (In a surviving copy of this booklet, the annotations of the original reader – writing the word 'Parliament' in the first house of the reference chart and 'Charles' in the tenth – show they had understood William's directions.)

Using the rules of mundane astrology, Lilly then analyzed the ingress chart (also known as an annual revolution or the *figura mundi* – 'world figure'). His judgement was that, overall, England's scheme of heaven for 1644 was 'averse to monarchy' – Parliament would have a better year than the King. But, he added, 'Both shall suffer and smart, I see no probability of concluding any peace … I am of the opinion there will be strong action and war all this whole year, and that there will be fighting enough and too much.'

Lilly had identified Mars as the planet signifying the parliamentary forces (this was because Mars was the ruler of the zodiac sign of Scorpio – the sign on the cusp of the first house). However, in the chart Mars was conjunct one of the four key angles of the horoscope, the *immum coeli* or IC (which was positioned at the start of the fourth house). This placement, on an angle, signalled clearly that the year ahead would be troublesome.

'Mars in any angle in *figura Mundi*, or year's revolution, excites men's minds to war and contention,' Lilly explained, highlighting how even if a nation was at peace, this placement of warmongering Mars 'provokes men to much law suits, the nobility to private duels, the gentry to envy'. The prospect of a martial year was lent weight, he added, by the Moon separating from a hard opposition aspect with

Mars: this presaged 'sadness, death, the effusion of blood'.

He dismissed any prospects that ongoing peace negotiations between the King and a faction within Parliament, the Independents, would come to anything, writing that 'all treaties end in smoke and vapour'. The proposals, he cautioned his audience, were too favourable to the King.

He then singled out June and July as particularly volatile months in which England should 'expect to hear of war, slaughter of men, division, towns besieged, some taken, some plundered ...' More specifically, he predicted, watch out for the period around 4 June when there would be 'much mischief, fighting and action' and the start of July: 'The first week in July may prove bloody ...'

His foresight was remarkable. The year of 1644 was one of the Civil War's bloodiest years of fighting: informal peace talks were not fruitful, the parliamentary army's advances forced Charles and most of his men to withdraw, on 3 June, from their stronghold in Oxford, and, on 2 July 1644, fighting began on Marston Moor in Yorkshire.

Marston Moor proved to be the greatest battle of the war, involving approximately 45,000 men, and the greatest ever fought on English soil. A decisive victory for the parliamentarian forces, it was a conflict in which the loss of life was immense – the royalists were reckoned to have lost at least 4,000 soldiers, with thousands more captured. The battle also marked the emergence of Oliver Cromwell, then lieutenant-general of horse.

The reaction inside the House of Commons to Lilly's maiden pamphlet was echoed outside its walls. *Merlinus Anglicus Junior* was an instant hit, with the first print run (typically between 1,250 and 1,500 copies) selling out within a few days; further print runs followed. Its resounding success was due to both its content and its style: Lilly's forecasts were compelling and accurate, his writing was eloquent and populist, and he had revealed some of the star science's secrets. What would this enthralling new prophet see and say next? The public and Parliament waited eagerly.

* * * *

Lilly was 'highly incensed'. It was the start of December 1644, a year since John Pym's death, and hours earlier he had been close to finishing *Merlinus Anglicus Junior* 1645. He had planned to take it to the licenser of almanacs later that day to make sure it was approved, at the printers and off the press before year-end.

But then a friend had arrived with some unpleasant news, and his plans for *Anglicus* had changed dramatically. Now, enraged and determined to vindicate his reputation, he had just committed treason and was about to broadcast that fact.

It was a pivotal moment in the ongoing Civil War. Parliament's forces had failed to capitalize on their Marston Moor victory: the King's men rallied in the following months and in late October avoided defeat at the second Battle of Newbury, despite being vastly outnumbered by Parliament's army; Charles entered Oxford in late November in triumph. Instead of sensing outright victory, the parliamentarians were back to negotiating peace terms with a recalcitrant monarch.

In the original version of his almanac, Lilly's overall prediction for the coming months had not offered much hope to either side. He had written: 'we must yet have more wrangling, quarrelling, bloodshed, slaughter of our fellow-subjects ... I can promise absolute victory to neither side this year ...'

He had also promised: 'I am resolved to stand close to the rules of art, without partiality to King or Parliament ... I cannot flatter, I will not: To mince my judgement, and deliver ambiguous stuff, is to lessen the validity of art. I stand upon the honour of my nation.'

These words were meant to show he did not want any part of the astrological propaganda war that was presently raging between pamphleteers with royalist sympathies and those on Parliament's side.

George Wharton, the most successful cavalier compiler, had begun the print battle over a year ago. Writing from the King's camp in Oxford and 'with his Majesty's command', he brazenly flew the royalist flag in his 1644 almanac. According to him, the heavens foretold that the King would triumph; the religious sects springing up would be suppressed; and leaders of the rebel forces would be hanged.

Putting his own spin on the first major encounter in the war – the Battle of Edgehill in Warwickshire (in which both sides had suffered heavy casualties) – Wharton lauded the King's courage and lambasted leading parliamentarians' cowardly ways, suggesting they were 'skulking in ... holes and sawpits'.

John Booker, who was now Parliament's licenser of astrological tracts, as well as its champion, had retaliated straightaway. Aiming to discredit the younger, less experienced astrologer, he described him as nothing but a 'court-parasite'; his booklet was 'a collection of untruths'; his 'reckoning up of victories at this and that place' were 'all false calculations'; his astrological analyses were flawed.

Why, he sneered, had Wharton chosen the ridiculous pseudonym Naworth (using an alias was a common practice among astrologers)? In Booker's opinion, his choice revealed the royalist seer was 'truly ... No-worth or a man worth nothing'. Please, he advised the public, 'I hope you will not bestow your money on so lying a pamphlet, or spend your time so vainly in reading such notorious untruths as this counterfeit Naworth would fain persuade you to believe ...'

After this initial heated exchange, the war of words escalated rapidly and became more personal. Wharton hit back, accusing Booker of being 'a rebel' who lived by 'cheating and lying', who wrote 'perfidious pamphlets' designed to beget 'fears and jealousies among the people'. He mocked Parliament's army for its large lower-class component: the 'many wood-mongers, fell-mongers, button-makers &c. which are your colonels and commanders. Your schismatical assembly of tailors, millers, cobblers and weavers ...'

Furthermore, Wharton warned, Booker had better watch his back. 'You began in blood, and I hope you shall (most part of you) make your end so ... Your railing against Majesty will not be forgotten, nor forgiven ... Have a care of your neck, for I have calculated your destiny ... Your death is not like to prove natural ...'

Lilly had hoped to avoid the name-calling and fisticuffs in ink. His aim in recent months had been to establish himself as the almanac author to read – based on his abilities as an astrologer. His approach was working: since July he had published a series of successful pamphlets.

All 1,800 copies of the first print run of *A Prophecy of the White King* – a controversial reworking of an ancient prophecy – were snapped up in just three days. In Lilly's reading of the white king prophecy, which his audience understood as referring to Charles I who at his coronation had worn white robes rather than the traditional purple, the denouement had Parliament overthrowing the King, and the monarch meeting a violent end. Readers loved it, and further editions were printed.

England's Prophetical Merlin also proved remarkably popular. Designed to whet all appetites, it was an editorially astute blend of sex and prophecy, which showcased a selection of real-life stories and celebrity insights, astrologically told. William had put a lot of thought into its content. He was a remarkably well-read magus: courtesy of his canny first marriage to an older, wealthy widow, he had had the time and the money to study astrology in greater depth than most, and he was making good use of this advantage.

He was following knowingly in the footsteps of a 16th-century Italian astrologer, Girolamo Cardano, who was catapulted from obscurity to cosmopolitan acclaim after his publications had titillated his audience with celebrity horoscopes revealing intimate secrets. Cardano's second bestseller, *De Judiciis Geniturarum* (1547), which Lilly owned, was in essence a forerunner of the true life stories devoured so zealously today. In it, Cardano offered a collection of birth horoscopes to stimulate all manner of palates: 'heretics, robbers, pederasts, sodomites ... philosophers ... the greatest physicians and diviners, and famous craftsmen'.

William's choices were similarly inspired. He covered the salacious: the gentlewoman who enquired whether 'she should have an aged man'; the elderly gent was keen, the maid was not and had her eye on a man of Mars – 'a captain or a soldier'. There was bread-and-butter stuff too: the trial of a lawsuit and a stolen goods query. The inclusion of John Pym's death chart added a note of celebrity, as well as cleverly broadcasting the author's relationship with Parliament.

His array of astral vignettes also worked as a wonderful advertisement for his talents. If folk knew their time and location of birth, *England's Prophetical Merlin* showed how Lilly could cast their nativity and provide a full natal chart analysis, highlighting all the major incidents in an individual's life as well as their allotted life span. He took his readers through the life of one of his clients – a gentleman who was unmarried 'but sufficiently potent'. This man, he forecast, would at the age of 52 suffer 'a virulent effluxion of matter' as a result of venereal disease, and would die on 5 December 1657.

While the case studies entertained and informed, it was Lilly's prediction of the King's prospects that provided the real meat – and prompted discussion. His forecast for his sovereign was shocking and stark: the Stuart dynasty, which had begun in 1603 when James acceded to the throne, was to be brought to its knees and changed irrevocably. Importantly, Lilly explained the astrological rationale for this. His judgement stemmed from conjunction theory: the analysis of the conjoining of the two superior planets Jupiter and Saturn in different zodiac signs over the centuries. As with all sidereal thinking, events on Earth were expected to mirror what was happening in the heavens.

The establishment of the Stuart line had coincided with a major conjunction of Jupiter and Saturn in the sign of Sagittarius (one of the three signs of the zodiac associated with fire). As this conjunction was the first to take place in the element of fire, subsequent meetings of these slow-moving planets (known as the *chronocrators*) were expected to occur in fire signs for the next 260 years.

However, in 1643, the cycle had been disturbed – Jupiter and Saturn met in the zodiac sign of Pisces, a water sign. For Lilly, this was an omen that 'the constant order of nature' was about to change.

'Times have no precedents,' he forecast, 'of the like excursion, or mutation (that ever I could read of) nor shall the ages in future see the like … there shall be a sensible disturbance, if not a final subversion, to those commonwealths and monarchies, that had originally their beginning … in 1603'.

January 1649, he foresaw, was the month and year to look out for. From 1647 onwards, he wrote, 'one monarchy begins to totter; and so by degrees God brings his purpose to perfection: but these judgements will be displeasing: for princes love not to hear of such matters … Yet in January 1649 … we have strong confidence of being quite cured of our distempers … we begin to smile: but monarchy is not in such great request as formerly …'

However, all was not quite lost for the Stuarts. 'In the years 1659 and 1660,' he concluded, 'our nobles and gentlemen root again … here's almost a new world, new laws, some new lords: now my country of England shall shed no more tears …'

While William's predictions had, from parliamentarians, garnered him the acclaim he sought, royalists reacted with fury and dismay. One cavalier complained that Parliament's piss-prophet 'led the commons of this kingdom, as bears ... are led by the nose with bagpipes before them'. Others noted that if Charles could have persuaded him to the King's cause, Lilly would have been worth half a dozen regiments; a royalist pamphleteer simply wished 'he were ours'.

George Wharton said much more in his almanac for 1644, which had just been published. Lilly, he declared was a 'pseudo-prophet' and 'an impudent senseless rebel' whose predictions were 'absurdities'; Booker was 'a licentious libeller'.

It was the news of these defamatory words that had brought William's friend, the physician Richard Napier, racing to the Corner House hours earlier. He thought (correctly) that Lilly would want to know immediately what was being said about him and to have the opportunity to respond in print. This was indeed William's reaction: he immediately began editing his manuscript of *Anglicus*.

Regarding Wharton's words, he retorted by writing, 'I will only contend in point of learning, and not in multiplicity of ill language,' and proceeded to highlight the many errors in the inexperienced astrologer's calculations. Then he moved on to his next, and bigger, target – the King. He was going to use his astrological know-how to give Parliament the upper hand during fighting.

Lilly was following the example of one of his most admired predecessors – Italy's Guido Bonatti, who was Europe's pre-eminent magus during the late Middle Ages and an expert in the art of war. In Bonatti's book *Liber introductorius ad iudica stellarum* ('A book of introduction to the judgements of the stars'), which Lilly knew well, he explained the rules of engagement for many conflict scenarios, including how to judge which side will win; whether there will be a battle between two armies; whether besieged castles or cities will fall; and whether a war is just.

Bonatti used his talents in advising his patron Count Guido da Montefeltro (a member of the Ghibelline political faction) on how best to defeat the Guelphs (the supporters of the Pope). Such was his success as a military tactician that the Guelph poet Dante Aligheri consigned both Bonatti and Montefeltro to Hell in his *Divine Comedy*. Bonatti was placed in the eighth circle of the imagined inferno, his head twisted round to face backwards for all eternity as a punishment for his ability, during life, to see into the future.

Lilly's sidereal battle strategy was based on exploiting his illegal knowledge of Charles I's nativity. Over the last few hours, he had used a technique, known as primary directions, to project the King's birth chart into the future. What he wanted to know was: was there a particular time during the year ahead that would be more difficult for the monarch? He found what he was looking for in early summer 1645.

In June, the key point in Charles's nativity known as the Ascendant, which was at 28° Leo, was approaching a tense and troublesome square aspect with malefic Mars. The astrological reading of this was that from the King's perspective this would not be a good time to fight. However, for the parliamentarian forces this was the point to push hard in battle; the stars revealed that then the heavens were on their side.

Lilly chose his words carefully. 'When we have probable hopes of good success beforehand promised us,' he wrote in his hastily amended almanac, 'it might encourage our soldiers to attempt greater actions: If the heavens be averse, more caution must be had, and fit election of times framed.'

In his predictions for the month of June, he forecast: 'The tenth or eleventh of June may be casually unlucky to a grandee of England, and he no mean one ... The heavens frown on our enemies for a while … Let us totally unite, there's great reason for it, and then if we fight, a victory steals upon us … Without doubt the day is ours, if God give us wisdom to husband time well.'

Satisfied with the new version of *Anglicus*, Lilly sat back and stretched. Tomorrow he would begin the process of publishing his pamphlet. But first there was something else he wanted to do. It was vital that Parliament and its army were aware of and acted on this specific prediction: could he influence the course of war more directly by alerting his circle of parliamentary and military contacts to 'this unlucky judgement'?

He would try Bulstrode Whitelocke first. Whitelocke was now at the heart of parliamentary politics. Weeks earlier, when new peace terms between Charles I and Parliament were proposed, it was Whitelocke who went to the King's encampment in Oxford to pursue further negotiations. And at the beginning of December, it was Whitelocke's support for Oliver Cromwell that stopped factions within Parliament from making moves against the up-and-coming soldier who had shown such prowess on Marston Moor.

Picking up his papers, Lilly stood and put on his cloak over his doublet; seconds later the door of the Corner House closed behind him. He would be at Westminster soon. Could Whitelocke's position as a respected and experienced Member of Parliament, and his role as Lilly's stalwart friend and supporter of astrology, come together to alter the course of the Civil War?

* * * *

On 14 June 1645, the New Model Army, Parliament's radically reorganized forces, faced the King in battle for the first time at Naseby in Leicestershire. Unaware of Lilly's advisory role within Parliament and dismissive of astrology's influence, modern historians have often been puzzled by the lead-up to Naseby. Why, it has been asked, when the New Model Army was at full strength and ready to fight since the end of April, did it wait until June to engage Charles?

Parliament's campaign has been criticized for being shapeless; old generals sitting on Parliament's Committee of Both Kingdoms have been blamed for the fact that May was a month of surprisingly little activity. Lilly's social circle and his audience knew better: the New Model Army was waiting until the astrologically auspicious time to strike.

Battle began at 11am. The New Model Army numbered between 14,500 and 17,000 men; Charles commanded a smaller force of 9,000 or 10,000 soldiers. Parliamentary infantry also had the advantage of higher ground. But the encounter could still have gone either way. On the field, strong leadership from the New Model Army commanders, Sir Thomas Fairfax and Oliver Cromwell, rallied their troops and ensured Parliament's triumph; above the battleground the stars shone favourably down for them. Lilly's sidereal military manoeuvres were a success.

While conflict was not yet over, the New Model Army's victory over Charles and his men was a decisive one and signalled the start of the end of the war. William Lilly's words had won the day for the parliamentarians and changed the course of English history.

Naseby altered the course of his fate too: he was now the nation's first media celebrity, famed in print and song throughout the land for his gift of foresight. But not everyone was happy to praise the new prophet; to some his rousing words were doing more harm than good. They began to plan their attack.

Chapter 2

The Society of Astrologers of London

$$\text{☽}$$

The Moon signifies home, history, the public and community,
the mother, fertility, the female principle and flux.
It is associated with silver, sea creatures, the willow,
pearls, harbours and ports, and the breast.

Less than two weeks after the parliamentary victory at the Battle of Naseby, Lilly was about to discover just how Janus-faced fame is. In the days since his accurate public prophecy of success for the New Model Army, he had been enjoying the benefits of his newfound celebrity – the good cheer and hearty handshakes bestowed on him, as well as more clients arriving at the Corner House.

But this time when he opened the door, William knew immediately that something was wrong. The stern-faced man on the doorstep was not a new customer keen to meet him; instead he had been sent by the Committee of Examinations's sergeant-at-arms to arrest him. Lilly's crime? In his recent almanacs he had dared to criticize Parliament and its improvised system of government by committee; someone had complained, and the Committee of Examinations, which had the power to search and seize scandalous and unlicensed pamphlets and apprehend their authors, wanted answers.

Serendipitously for Lilly, as he was being marched to Westminster, he met a group of MP friends: Philip Stapleton, Christopher Wray, Denzil Holles and Robert Reynolds. Seeing his worried look, they reassured him they would attend his hearing and do all they could to help. But, they warned, the committee's chair was the unpopular Miles Corbet, who was notorious for his arbitrary and inquisitorial approach, and, they had heard, wanted to punish Lilly soundly.

William's friends were true to their word. As the hearing began, Corbet was called forward to explain why Lilly had been seized, and Reynolds quickly sat himself down in the chair: with Reynolds now chairman, there was a chance to counter and control Corbet's capricious manner.

Corbet's opening sally concerned the Commissioners of the Excise – the officials coordinating the collection, via local committees and sub-officers, of the much-loathed tax on staples such as meat and salt, which had been introduced two years earlier to raise war funds. Waving aloft a copy of *Merlinus Anglicus Junior*, Corbet announced that the pamphlet he was holding contained many scandalous passages about the Commissioners of the Excise.

Lilly held his breath. He had commented, in his central forecast for 1645, on the financial burden common folk were feeling and had offered his prediction that this would lead to unrest. 'Our Commonwealth or Parliament shall have vast expenses,' he had written, 'and exhaust the kingdoms, I reassure, almost to beggary, that the vulgar sort of people ... shall be extremely oppressed with heavy and burdensome payments, almost to their utter impoverishment.'

England's horoscope for the year ahead foretold 'their disquieted souls, and aptness to stir up their spirits against the gentry, and their new lords, called committee-men.' Expect turmoil within 'our Parliament and their sub-officers and committees,' he added; 'you shall see pretty sport, and find many unsound and faithless officers purged, scourged, cleansed ...'

However, when Corbet read aloud one of the offending passages, he discovered that his colleagues saw things differently. The members of the committee, instead of agreeing that Lilly's words denounced the top officials, took the forecast to refer to the errors of mere local sub-officers. Turning to Lilly, they asked him which interpretation was correct; the latter was the true meaning, he sensibly affirmed.

Corbet tried again. William had also included several remarks about the delayed payment of soldiers – at that period the army received wages about 75 per cent of the time. One of his comments read: 'God bless us from men and soldiers malcontented; men that have their wages ill paid, and yet have fought valiantly ... Let all officers that have dipped their fingers in silver commands, give account ... Let us pay deserving men, cowards can pay themselves.'

The passage Corbet wanted to read to the tribunal said, 'In the name of the Father, Son and Holy Ghost, will not the Excise pay the soldiers?' However, flustered by not getting the response he had hoped for the first time, he faltered, asking instead, 'will not the eclipse pay soldiers?' The occupants of the room erupted into hearty laughter; quashed, Corbet fell silent. It was not going his way.

By this time, news had travelled around the Commons that the celebrated star-gazer William Lilly had been apprehended and the tribunal chamber was packed with MPs – some keen to hear Lilly speak, others eager to grasp the chance to make trouble for him. When chairman Reynolds declared, 'Have you any more against Mr Lilly?', his enemies got their moment.

First to speak was the solicitor for the Excise. Standing up, he announced the astrologer was to blame for his house being burnt down and his fellow Commissioners of Excise being publicly abused – the latter had been 'pulled by their clothes in the [Royal] Exchange', the city's centre of commerce. This had all happened, he said, since the publication of Lilly's pamphlet, the *Starry Messenger*.

It soon became apparent, though, that the man from the Excise was lying. The *Starry Messenger* was Lilly's most recent publication and his most talked about yet. In it, he forecast that the King would not be able to hold on to the town of Leicester after its recent sacking by Prince Rupert and his men. He was correct: Leicester had been stormed and had surrendered to Parliament on 18 June.

The *Starry Messenger* also contained the prediction that the New Model Army would secure 'an absolute victory', and had then, memorably, been published on the very day that the army achieved this – at the Battle of Naseby on 14 June. But when the solicitor of the Excise was questioned about when his house was destroyed and the aldermen abused, he answered that this had happened twelve days before Naseby.

Hearing this, acting chairman Reynolds pounced. Lilly's pamphlet, he reminded the tribunal, launched 'The very day of Naseby fight, nor need he be ashamed of writing it, I had it daily as it came forth of the press.' The MP Sir Robert Pym then weighed in, saying: 'What a lying fellow art thou to abuse us so.'

The next to stand was a merchant, Mr Bassell. Inveighing bitterly against Lilly, Bassell demanded the astrologer's books be burnt. The reason for his anger lay in his religion (he was a Presbyterian), and the current fight for religious control of the parliamentary cause.

Charles I's autocratic ecclesiastical policy had been one of the triggers for Civil War, and the eve of the war saw the Anglican state church with its system of episcopacy – rule by bishops appointed by the monarch – collapse. The question then, which remained still, was what system of church government would replace it? In the 17th century, this was a vital issue: despite the burgeoning press, the pulpit was still the key means of winning (and binding) human minds.

Presbyterians wanted a national church based around presbyteries, where decision-making, such as the election of ministers, lay with representatives of local congregations and where membership of a congregation was determined by an individual's place of domicile. Their position on many topics, including freedom of worship and astrology, was typically one of intolerance (the church's general view of astrology was that it was an impious art that undermined the concept of free will and trespassed on godly terrain in divining the future).

However, since 1644, support for Independent congregations had been growing within Parliament and the army. The Independents rejected the national structure of the church and instead supported like-minded Christians gathering voluntarily, rather than according to geography, and these Independent congregations choosing their own pastors. The Presbyterians presently held the majority within Parliament, but it was the tolerant Independents, who counted Cromwell among their number and encompassed the growing number of radical religious sects, who were gaining ground.

In the wake of Naseby, the question was which faction within Parliament – supporters of the Independents or the Presbyterians – could be the source of authority; which could negotiate a peace agreement with the King and take ecclesiastical control of the nation?

It was a critical period and Bassell was annoyed that Lilly, in his 1645 almanac, had declared his opposition to Presbyterianism and his support for church reform and 'settling the liberties of the subject'. William's dislike of the Presbyterians was not without reasonable cause: week after week, Presbyterian ministers preached lengthy sermons against the evils of astrology and Lilly, in particular. In response, William poured scorn in his almanac on 'the invective divine, who sometimes consumes a precious hour in confutation of astrology'.

Fortunately for Lilly, the committee did not like Bassell's tone and remained unconvinced by the merchant's arguments. 'You smell more of a citizen than a scholar,' dismissed MP Francis Drake. With no more charges to be dealt with, Lilly was led out of the tribunal chambers while the Committee of Examinations, led by Reynolds, deliberated over its verdict.

Standing outside the hearing, William considered his position. He knew his friends would do all they could to try to ensure he remained a free man able to continue to broadcast his prophecies, but he was deeply concerned he would be gagged.

He was right to be worried. Parliament did pursue its outspoken critics and those espousing non-conformist views. During the summer of 1645, the Company of Stationers was seeking to shut down the underground presses used by prolific pamphleteer Richard Overton; weeks earlier, in June, Miles Corbet had been on the offensive against religious and political radical John Lilburne (who in July would be imprisoned for his critical comments).

Comments against the King did not go unpunished either. Marchamont Nedham, the editor of the parliamentarian newsbook *Mercurius Britanicus*, would be imprisoned in August for publishing passages 'scandalous to the King's person' – he had mocked Charles I's speech impediment (the monarch was known to stutter). The newsbook's printer and its licenser would be incarcerated too.

Prognostications Lilly had made recently about Charles I had the potential to place him in even more trouble. Both in his almanac for 1645 and in the *Starry Messenger*, he had again acted illegally by calculating his sovereign's nativity – and this time he had revealed how the position of the Sun in the King's birth chart augured that he was in great danger of a sudden and violent death.

In Charles's natal horoscope, the Sun was adjacent to the fixed star *Cor Scorpii*, which, as well as presaging fatality, was said to make men self-destructive as a result of their own stubbornness. When placed next to the luminaries or lights (the Sun and the Moon), it portended honour and riches that end in disgrace, downfall and violent death.

Because it was too dangerous for Lilly to state this judgement directly, he had found a way of cloaking his comments. Instead of discussing the position of the Sun in Charles's nativity, he had analysed an unexpected celestial event that occurred on the King's birthday the previous year (19 November 1644) – the appearance of two mock suns in the sky flanking the real Sun.

Mock suns, sometimes called sun dogs and today known as parhelia, are natural phenomena typically seen when the sun is low, and result from the interplay of sunlight with ice crystals. They are now understood as a normal occurrence for a bright, wintry day – commonplace in late November in England.

In Lilly's era, though, they were another portent to be deciphered. They were the starry messengers of his pamphlet, which featured on its front cover a spectacular woodcut illustration of the three suns with a rainbow above them (PLATE 2, PAGE 38).

However, as he expected his readers to appreciate, when he discussed the meaning of the position of the sun dogs on 19 November 1644 (at 8° Sagittarius and conjunct the Scorpion's Heart), he was also explaining the significance of the placement of the Sun in Charles's nativity (also at 8° Sagittarius and conjunct the Scorpion's Heart).

In the *Starry Messenger*, he prophesised: 'Are not both the lights, in our scheme, with or near *Cor Scorpii*, a most violent fixed star which usually (if we believe antiquity or experience) threatens sudden and violent death ... He or she of any great family, that hath either the Sun or Moon, or both, with this star, in the radix of their nativities, are threatened hereby ... Look to your selves; here's some monstrous death towards you ...'

In his 1645 almanac, he forecast: 'The last 19 of November,

PLATE 2 The front cover of *The Starry Messenger*
(reproduced with permission of the Bodleian Libraries,
The University of Oxford, Ashm.548(5), Title Page)

three suns appeared: some unheard of action ensues ... Is any grandee surprised, captivated, or made shorter by the head?'

He then went a step further. He had noticed that a solar eclipse in August 1645 occurred at 28° Leo – the degree of the Ascendant in Charles's natal chart. 'What great one soever thou art of England, or of any nation of Europe, that hast the 27 or 28 of Leo ascending at thy birth,' he predicted, 'to thee I say, thou art in great danger of death ... I am not idle, but thou art mad, and out of thy wits, if thou dost not beware in time ... I know the nativities of two princes or great persons, to whom this eclipse portends either destruction, or many fearful calamities: Their names I hold fit to be concealed, &c.'

So, as he waited to hear the Committee of Examinations's outcome, his concerns for his safety were justified. Although his friends' efforts resulted in his being discharged on this occasion, less than a week later another complaint was made and he was arrested again.

Once more Robert Reynolds and Philip Stapleton stood for him, persuading the committee that the matter was both frivolous in nature and malicious in intent – 'presented by a choleric person to please a company of clowns' – and once again they brought about his release. But this time William had had enough. It was time to put into action his strategy to ensure he would not, and could not, be silenced, ever.

* * * *

Stepping back, William breathed out and relaxed, the good wishes ringing in his ears. Despite feeling so unwell (he had heart palpitations and melancholia), the business had gone splendidly. The company of men in front of him on this Sunday at the end of February 1647 had agreed to come together at least twice a year to hold a 'Mathematician's Feast' to celebrate and progress their profession.

They had also decided to listen to an appropriate lecture at each meeting, had appointed a steward to organize future proceedings, and had approved Lilly's suggestion that Bulstrode Whitelocke be the patron of the newly-formed Society of Astrologers of London. Despite their differing allegiances, they had managed to avoid any disputes around King, Parliament or army; William hoped they would continue to do so.

Looking around the room in Gresham College, Bishopsgate, home to the city's first institute of higher learning, Lilly was happy to see so many of his peers. As news of the society spread, his hope was soon to see above 40 or 50 astrologers attending. Tonight, old friends were there: fellow pamphleteer John Booker, his drinking companion William Pool, and physician and tutor Nicolas Fiske.

Others he knew on a professional basis: astrologer physician Richard Saunders was a protégé, while Nicholas Culpeper was master of the decumbiture – a horoscope of the moment a person is taken ill. He had also spotted mathematician and clergyman William Oughtred, whom he had recently helped avoid being thrown out of his parsonage in Albury, Surrey.

A new friend was present too: the royalist lawyer Elias Ashmole. The two men had come in together and had spoken before the start of the meeting. The younger man, who was 29, was worrying as usual about his health. He was concerned, he told Lilly, about two large boils which had broken out four days earlier on the right-hand side of his throat – one directly beneath his ear, the other a little lower.

But, Ashmole confided, what had been occupying him for most of that day and the previous night were his bowels. He had been suffering from painful constipation and at seven o'clock that morning had taken an electuary, a potion of powdered herbs in syrup, in a bid to move his humours down. Four hours later, when the draught had not yet worked its effects, he looked to the heavens for answers regarding his 'late stool' and found them in Saturn. The planet of obstructions was in an antagonistic opposition aspect to the Moon (which was understood as the chief determinant of the body's fluctuating humours).

But within half an hour, the electuary had begun to work and was then so effective that just after midday Ashmole felt the need to draw up a horary figure of heaven asking 'whether I shall go to the Feast of Mathematicians at Gresham College'. Like all his illnesses, the boils, constipation and diarrhoea had necessitated entries in his diary. Later that night, he would record, 'The last stool I had this day was at 6 a clock having in all 7 stools'.

William liked Ashmole enormously, despite the difference in their ages and their political stance. The young man's intelligence, and enthusiasm and love for the stellar science, were heartening to him. But what did worry him was Ashmole's close relationship with fellow royalist George Wharton, who was still railing in print against him at every opportunity.

Lilly's hope for the Society of Astrologers of London was that meeting as a guild would create a supportive community of like-minded colleagues and begin to improve professional standards. He had long felt a lack of intellectual vigour within his trade (which was in part a consequence of the stringent regulations controlling astrologers and almanacs in England since Elizabethan times).

During his first years of studying the mantic art, he had taken the time to get to know as many of the metropolis's astromancers as he could; and, on the whole, he was not impressed. Most men were past their prime (in terms of both age and judgement), the vast majority were mediocre and only a couple gained his admiration.

Captain Bubb, who worked south of the river in Lambeth Marsh answering horary questions, exemplified the rogues within the profession. Judged on appearances, he seemed a fine fellow – he was well-spoken and extremely handsome. But shortly after William made his acquaintance, Bubb's dishonesty was revealed when one wronged customer, a butcher, complained.

The butcher had consulted Bubb after being robbed of £40 on his way to a fair. In response, Bubb promised to find the thief, but asked for £10 up-front to help him do so. After pocketing the down payment, the captain declared that the heavens had told him the culprit would be at a particular place at midnight; all the butcher had to do was lie in wait.

The butcher did so, and sure enough, at midnight, a man appeared riding a horse at full gallop. The butcher charged, knocking down and seizing both the man and the horse, and then took them to the next town – he had his felon.

But then the full story came out. The man he had seized was Captain Bubb's manservant John: it had all been a set-up. Bubb was indicted for the fraud and was found guilty and pilloried – locked by the neck and wrists in a wooden frame and jeered at on market day in regular six-hour bouts.

Former soldier Alexander Hart was another scoundrel. Handsome, elderly and charming, he lived in Houndsditch in east London, close to the city wall. Lilly visited him on a number of occasions, bringing with him horary questions he was considering, but Hart made mistakes in judging each scheme. Shortly afterwards, Hart was arrested for cheating a young city man out of his money – he had failed to conjure up a spirit and had refused to return the client's £20 deposit.

In contrast, cleric William Bredon was an honest soul. The rector of the parish church of St Michael & All Angels in Thornton, Buckinghamshire, was an intelligent fellow with a gift for interpreting nativities using a method espoused by the ancient Greek astrologer Ptolemy. But Bredon was a drinker and had such a terrible nicotine addiction 'that when he had no tobacco, he would cut the bell ropes, and smoke them'.

Dr Jeffrey Neve and Dr Richard Delahay (who practised under the pseudonym of Dr Ardee) were both astrologer physicians in their fifties when Lilly met them, but although they were honest, William found them of 'moderate judgement'. Even his friend William Pool was nothing but a 'nibbler' – one who had not mastered the art. Pool and Lilly became friends because Pool 'was very good company for drolling' – he was witty and always made Lilly laugh.

Pool's many different jobs – he had had at least seventeen – were often the source of his humour. He had worked as a gardener, plasterer, bricklayer, apparitor (attendant to a civil or ecclesiastical officer), and sometimes drew linen – making handkerchiefs and coifs (close-fitting caps). He also fancied himself as a poet.

On one occasion, Pool was accused of being in the company of lewd folk in a tavern where a silver cup was stolen. Hearing that a justice of the peace, Sir Thomas Jay, had issued a warrant for his arrest, Pool quickly packed all his astrology books in a small trunk and escaped to Westminster to lie low. Some months later, on receiving the welcome news that Sir Jay was dead, Pool found out where he was buried, visited his grave, defecated upon it and commemorated his act in verse:

Here lyeth buried Sir Thomas Jay Knight,
Who being dead, I upon his grave did shite.

Even Lilly's first (and only) tutor, John Evans, who had 'the most piercing judgement', was 'the veriest knave'. They had been introduced by a mutual acquaintance fifteen years ago, when William was approaching his thirtieth birthday. The former clergyman lived and worked in Gunpowder Alley, just off Shoe Lane and not far from the Corner House, and during six weeks in the spring of 1632, Lilly had spent as much time as possible with him – watching him cast horaries for clients and listening to his spellbinding tales of how to conjure spirits (Evans had 'studied the dark arts').

On first meeting Evans, he thought his tutor was 'the most perfect Saturnine person' his eyes had ever beheld – that is, the Welshman's physiognomy and temperament were redolent of the attributes associated with Saturn. He was beetle-browed, flat-nosed and full-lipped, a shock of grey-black curling stiff hair rose above a broad forehead and downward-scowling eyes, and his body was squat, with thick shoulders and feet that splayed out.

Unfortunately for the lapsed cleric, the very aspect of horary at which he shone – answering questions about lost or stolen property – was illegal. The 'Against Conjuration, Witchcraft and Dealings with Evil and Wicked Spirits' Act of 1604 stated that people were liable for prosecution if they 'take upon him or them[selves] by witchcraft, enchantment, charm or sorcery to tell or declare in what place any treasure or gold or silver should or might be found or had in the earth or other secret places, or where goods or things lost or stolen should be found or become'. For a first offence, the punishment was a year in prison, plus being pilloried; a second offence carried a death sentence. Evans had fled from his previous practice outside London in order to avoid prosecution for giving 'judgement upon things lost'.

Lilly had had doubts about his teacher from the beginning. His first sight of him had been with the latter lying hungover in his bed, struggling to wake up and focus. Unfortunately, the more time he spent with Evans, the less he liked him: the older man was not only a drunk, but was addicted to debauchery, was often abusive and quarrelsome, was seldom without a black eye or one or two bruises and made the majority of his income from the sale of dubious and dangerous home-made remedies. (Evans would later be accused of killing two of his customers with his antimonial cups – purgative cups made from the toxic chemical antimony.)

Their relationship ended abruptly and acrimoniously after William saw his tutor deliberately give an incorrect judgement to a female customer. Evans's explanation was that although it was the wrong answer astrologically, it was the right one for his business. 'I judged to please the woman,' he said; 'if I had not done so, she would have given me nothing, and I have a wife and family to provide for.' Turning away, Lilly vowed never to speak with him again; he knew then that this was not how he wanted to practise.

Out of all the astrologers of whom he made the acquaintance during the first half of the 1630s, only two gained his regard – John Booker and the Reverend Richard Napier of Great Linford (the uncle of the friend who warned Lilly in 1644 about Wharton's libellous words). Napier, in particular, was an inspiration: he had been celebrated for his work as an astrological physician and had known the infamous 16th-century London magus Simon Forman. Sadly, Napier had died not long after Lilly had met him.

Today, Lilly could count the astrologers he respected on one hand: himself, Booker, Culpeper, Nicholas Fiske (though he lacked confidence), and perhaps Ashmole – one of the few youthful fellows (which was another problem for the profession). This was not enough if the star science and its practitioners were to thrive as he wished.

But there was another, more personal and pressing reason why the creation of the Society of Astrologers of London was critical and timely: William was afraid, and had been for some time, that 1647 would be the year he died. Like any accomplished astrologer, he analyzed his own natal chart and, using the primary directions technique, progressed his geniture forwards in time to see what each year promised. For 1647, he had seen that his Ascendant by direction was in a hard square aspect with maleficent Mars and the Moon. This was an ominous sign.

He committed his foresight to print. Three years earlier, in *England's Prophetical Merlin,* he described 1647 as 'that year which afflicts me', and prophesied that during those twelve months 'I shall be in great danger of my life'. So far, the attacks had merely been verbal: the number of ministers calling for his quill pen to be put down was on the increase, while 'lewd Mercurys' (news sheets) printed in London and Oxford continued to abuse him. As he put it: 'The Presbyterians were, in their pulpits, as merciless as the cavaliers in their pamphlets.'

But his health was suffering too. Like many others, last year's poor harvest had taken its toll and he had scurvy, as well as problems with his spleen and palpitations. He had also started to feel melancholic again, a feeling he had experienced previously in his early thirties, and which was then the result of working too hard and spending too much time exploring the dark arts (he had since burnt his 'books which instructed these curiosities').

Now, though, as the inaugural meeting of the Society of Astrologers came to a close, it was time to repair to the White Hart to raise a tankard to the new venture. However, he could not stay till late, for tomorrow he had to give further help to William Pennington, who was still under threat of sequestration.

This time, Pennington had asked him to tell a committee hearing about the misdemeanours committed by one of his enemies – Isaac Antrobus, a rich, heavy-drinking parson. Lilly was going to swear that Antrobus 'had baptized a cock, and called him Peter', had had sexual intercourse with both a mother and her daughter, had been tied up by a woman by 'his privy members unto a manger in a stable', was 'a continual drunkard' and 'never preached'.

Despite Antrobus being a champion of Parliament, William was hopeful he could sway proceedings in Pennington's favour, and had arranged for an abundance of his friends to be there to assist him. There was not much he would not do to help those he cared for: he had had the mettle as a 22-year-old servant to use scissors to perform a makeshift mastectomy when his mistress, who was dying of breast cancer, had begged him to. He was confident he could win over the Committee of Plundered Ministers, although he was still worried about what the rest of the year would bring.

* * * *

Gazing at the picture, Lilly smiled broadly. He was pleased with what he saw (PLATE 3, PAGE 48). Staring up at him was a dashing and debonair man in his prime, dressed in his finery. Long brown hair curled down to his shoulders, a wavy fringe fell forwards across his forehead framing his deep brown eyes and aquiline nose, and he sported the newly popular Van Dyke beard (made famous in the 21st century by the actor Johnny Depp).

The gentleman's clothes underscored his striking looks: a white damask collar, a pearl-white brooch and white shirtsleeves contrasted starkly with the fashionable black cloak slung around his shoulders and dark doublet underneath. This was William in his prime.

The image, commissioned from the well-known British engraver William Marshall, was rich in symbolism and history, its setting proclaiming key messages about its subject's professional status and power. It was a fair likeness too, even down to the scar on the brow of his nose from when Lilly had contracted measles at the age of four.

Readers of the publication that this portrait would grace would see him seated at a table in front of a window, his right hand resting lightly on the top of a celestial sphere or star globe, used by star-gazers to compute the times of the rising and setting of stars and their point

PLATE 3 William Lilly aged 45
(reproduced with permission of the Bodleian Libraries,
The University of Oxford, 939e.529, Frontispiece)

of culmination. His stance seemed to say: 'this, the heavens and their movements, are in my dominion'.

On the table in front of him were other tools of his trade. To his far left was a quill and stand; next, a sidereal textbook, its pages open to reveal the astrological glyphs for the seven planets, the twelve zodiac signs and the five planetary aspects. His left hand held a piece of paper with the outline of a figure of heaven on it. Above the empty horoscope, the phrase *'Aetatis* 45' announced his age to be 45. The words in the chart's central square – *Non cogunt* ('They do not compel') – declared much more.

This was William's philosophy of astrology: he believed the stars inclined but did not compel. What he meant by this was that while planetary movements unveiled happenings on earth, people could still act to change their fate – for example, by asking their god to intercede or by changing their course of action. Destiny, for Lilly, was negotiable. In his opinion, understanding the language of the heavens elevated individuals to be directors of their fortune, not mere servants of chance – and he was their conduit.

In the engraving, the scene visible through the window behind him was mysterious – conveying both a magical and pastoral aura. A great horoscope hung high in the heavens, while birds flew above a shepherd herding his sheep and a fisherman on the far bank of the river, and beyond lay a village with a church and steeple. At the base of the portrait was the identification in Latin: 'William Lilly, astrologer, born Leicestershire 1st May 1602.'

The backdrop was cryptic: its symbolism spoke to both Lilly's background and religion. His roots lay in the country. He was a farmer's boy from the village of Diseworth in the county of Leicestershire, who could not drive a plough or endure country labour and was, according to his father, William senior, 'good for nothing'. After his mother, Alice, died, and his father ended up in debtor's jail, he left his brother and sister behind and walked to London a penniless eighteen-year-old.

The sky chart above him showed a meeting of Saturn and Jupiter in the final degrees of Pisces – a position they had occupied in 1643, and which he had forecast announced the downfall of Charles Stuart. 'This is where I come from, and this is what I am and will be known for,' was one interpretation of his image and its setting.

Another take was allegorical. Current thinking suggested that the birth of Jesus Christ had been heralded by a conjunction of Saturn and Jupiter in 7 BCE on the Pisces-Aries cusp – the point where the sign of Pisces (depicted by two fish) ends and that of Aries (the ram) begins. The rustic imagery, showing the Fisher of Souls and the Shepherd of Men, echoed this deeper spiritual meaning. It spoke to the fact that the portrait was to be the frontispiece for a work entitled *Christian Astrology* – Lilly's first book.

William had begun *Christian Astrology* over eighteen months ago (as part of his plan to make sure that he and astrology would not be silenced). Now, in June 1647, he was close to finishing its third and final volume. His aim was straightforward: to produce a comprehensive guidebook that would be 'very convenient for learners'.

Book One, *An Introduction to Astrology*, taught the basics of the art: how to use an ephemeris and how to erect a figure of heaven. It also described astrology's symbolic language, outlining the meanings of different planetary placements and aspects.

For example, Lilly explained how Venus in Taurus signified 'a quiet man, not given to law, quarrel or wrangling … loving mirth in his words and actions, cleanly in apparel … prone to venery, oft entangled in love-matters, zealous in their affections, musical, delighting in baths and all honest merry meetings, or masks and stage-plays …'

But Venus in Scorpio was a different matter. 'Then he is riotous, expensive, wholly given to looseness and lewd companies of women

... coveting unlawful beds, incestuous, an adulterer; fanatical, a mere skipjack, of no faith, no repute, no credit; spending his means in alehouses, taverns and amongst scandalous, loose people ...'

Book Two, *The resolution of all manner of questions and demands*, taught the techniques for reading and judging a horary chart. He covered all types of questions and drew on all aspects of his life to do so: there were carefully selected examples from his clients, the war years and his personal life (he revealed how he was forced to pay too high a price for the Corner House in 1634).

One of these queries came from Elias Ashmole. He had been spending a lot more time with Elias recently: his friend had translated some prophecies for him for his most recent pamphlet, *World's Catastrophe*; he had helped devise 'the form and fashions' of some of the horary charts in *Christian Astrology*; and, a few days ago, under an auspicious aspect between the Moon and Mercury, he had begun drawing up the textbook's index.

Lilly was concerned for Elias, though. The young gentleman was a highly intelligent mercurial person with many passions, including alchemy, and the question he had brought to him at the end of last month was, 'Whether he should obtain the philosopher's stone? Or, that elixir by which such wonders are performed?'

Unfortunately for Ashmole, the horary indicated that his search would be 'in vain and to no purpose': William judged 'that he erred in his materials or composition, working on things too terrene or of too gross or heavy a substance'. But what was more worrying was that the horoscope augured a spell of sickness approaching; 'have a care of your health,' William had warned.

Ashmole's case study (presented anonymously) was one of only two he had included where the outcome was still unknown. The other centred on the ongoing political crisis and was sure to generate publicity for his book. The query was, 'If Presbytery shall stand?', and it had been asked a few months earlier, on 11 March at 4.45pm, by a Member of Parliament, Thomas Middleton. His question about what system of church government the country would end up with was one that still troubled everyone, but it currently had additional resonance for those in the army, as Middleton was.

At the time, the Presbyterians in Parliament were petitioning to disband the New Model Army in a bid to reduce public expenditure, and because the army represented a potential obstacle to their aims. In opposition, the increasingly discontented and politicized army and the radical Independents were exploring the opportunity to come together in order to try and fulfil their own ambitions.

Meanwhile, the King, who had been in captivity since surrendering in May 1646, had been uncompromising in all peace talks. He was opposed to both a Presbyterian settlement and to relinquishing control of the militia (just as he had been at the outbreak of war in 1642).

Now, as July approached, the situation remained unresolved and a new war seemed possible. The Presbyterians held control of Parliament and the militia in London, and were discussing a peace settlement with Charles I that would give them what they wanted. But in response, the New Model Army, acting on orders from Oliver Cromwell, had seized control of the King, published its manifesto of political aims and was currently marching slowly on London.

Lilly's judgement for Middleton was that the Presbyterians would not prevail in England. In *Christian Astrology*, he wrote: 'the Presbytery shall be too strict, sullen and dogged for the English constitutions … the gentry, or supremest people of this kingdom, do in part decline from the severity of the too austere clergy or Presbytery, mistrusting a thraldom rather than a freedom to ensue hereupon.'

The 'Countryman', he added, would be the lead player in the dance against them, the main reason why Presbytery 'will not stand or continue'. The 'Countryman', as Middleton and the nation knew, was the epithet for Cromwell, the former gentleman-farmer from the Fens of East Anglia.

In Lilly's opinion, this particular horary was also one in which 'posterity may see there's some verity in astrology': this was because he judged that it also foretold Charles I's demise by the end of the decade. 'Three whole years from hence shall not pass,' he had written, ' 'ere authority itself, or some divine providence inform our understanding with a way in discipline or government, either more near to the former purity of the primitive times, or more beloved of the whole kingdom of England ... For some time we shall not discover what shall be established, but all shall be even as when there was no king in Israel ...'

Forecasts aside, the most striking aspect of *Christian Astrology* was that it was the first comprehensive astrology text to be written in English, rather than Latin. This was a calculated move on Lilly's part. His ground-breaking guidebook was composed in the vernacular, with a mass-market readership in mind, because he wanted to reform astrology education radically.

From its beginnings, astrology had always been part of a nation's elite culture. In its very early days, the magi of the ancient Near East (the *umannu*) held the most important civil job in the realm: they were the conduit between heaven and Earth. There were only two routes to this highly sought-after position: be born into one of the upper class families, which monopolized the office of the *umannu* from generation to generation, or prove yourself as one of the kingdom's intelligentsia. This state of affairs would not change much for millennia.

Since medieval times in the Western world, the study of astrology had been firmly based in the universities: the star science was an integral part of both a medical degree and the liberal arts curriculum (within the quadrivium of arithmetic, geometry, astronomy and music). But its specialized academic status meant that it was taught in Latin, astrology textbooks were written in Latin and consequently the mantic art was only understood and practised by society's intellectual elite (typically those privileged enough to have a university education).

In the first half of the 17th century, the celestial science remained a university subject and its practitioners, in the main, came from the ruling classes. Even if aspiring adepts could arrange to be tutored by an experienced magus (as Lilly had), they still needed a certain level of education: without a working knowledge of Latin they could not read the necessary textbooks. Consequently, the profession continued to be a closed shop to the majority of society (just as medicine, law and divinity were).

William vehemently opposed the cloistering of knowledge in any form. He had felt what it was like to be excluded: he had been a bright lad, and excelled at Latin while at grammar school, but was abruptly prevented from attending Cambridge University after his mother's sudden death and his father's plunge into penury.

One of his chief criticisms about his country's 'malevolent, churlish and envious clergy' was their attempt to protect their elevated position in society by withholding wisdom from the masses. In *World's Catastrophe*, he described these divines as 'men of envy! that for so many ages, have envied mankind the knowledge of learning, that formerly cloistered up books, and suffered them to perish in your closets unopened, because all should be ignorant but yourselves.'

His democratic desire to open up the divinatory art to all, whatever their social or educational status, was a timely one. It resonated with contemporary calls from London radicals, led by John Lilburne and Richard Overton, to reform the legal system by using English, rather than Latin, in law courts. It also came two years before Nicholas Culpeper would challenge the closed shop of pharmacy and medicine by 'Englishing' the College of Physicians's

Pharmacopoeia Londinensis (the College's directory of how to make its pills and potions).

However, Lilly had also written *Christian Astrology* because he had long thought that the ill will some felt for astrology stemmed from a basic lack of understanding of it. He wrote in his 1645 almanac about his belief that the source of 'the small conceit and opprobrious judgement the English nation have of astrology' was 'the want of books fitted for the capacities of our English', rather than 'any wilful defect in their understandings'.

At that time, he had promised: 'I will write not only now, but, if God spare me life, I will make this art hereafter perceptible to the meanest, and useful for every vulgar capacity, I hope to the content of the whole kingdom.'

Today, with the elaborate, engraved frontispiece completed, he was moving another step closer to fulfilling his promise of strengthening the profession and its reputation. He hoped to finish the third volume of *Christian Astrology*, on how to judge nativities, within weeks and had just begun composing an introduction 'to the reader'.

In the latter, he was going to describe how he came to be an astrologer. But how much of his background should he reveal? Would it be wise to explain how he had originally been a servant at the Corner House, and that his transformation to master there had come about by secretly wedding his deceased employer's wife?

* * * *

At the end of August 1647, the Corner House was silent, its door closed to all customers. Inside Lilly and his wife were sombre and scared. The house was shut up because plague had struck it: at the start of August a first servant had died; days earlier another maidservant

55

had passed away. Now the remaining occupants waited to find out their fate.

Lilly had predicted in his 1647 almanac that it would be a plague year. However, his view was that 'the sickness, which we call the plague' would not 'much affect us'. He was correct in terms of an overarching perspective. There was a plague epidemic, but this was not one of the more severe years – there were 3,597 deaths in London (representing under a third of all deaths) in a population approaching 460,000. In contrast, the plague to come in 1665 would kill up to 100,000 citizens.

Fears about the plague had heightened existing tensions within the city. The New Model Army presently occupied the metropolis and had done so since the start of the month. Working together with the Independents, including the recently formed Levellers movement led by John Lilburne, Richard Overton and William Walwyn, the army was now irrefutably a political body and was beginning to openly pursue a settlement for the nation.

The struggle for control of Parliament was bitter: the Presbyterians were still holding the majority, despite the ousting of eleven of their members, but the army and the Independents were pushing for a further purge, which would hand power over to them. Meanwhile, with the parliamentary alliance in tatters and a resurgence in royalist feeling in some quarters, the King had seen the chance to improve his political prospects. He reopened discussions with the army and requested being moved to be held prisoner at his house at Hampton Court, where he would be more comfortable and, he hoped, less closely guarded.

Inside the Corner House, Lilly was exhausted. He was determined to finish *Christian Astrology* before he met his fate, whatever it was. Days earlier he had finished composing the introduction to his work; only the nativities section was incomplete. He had decided to tell his readers what was happening and had apologized for any mistakes made in the final parts of the manuscript because it was 'written when my family and self were in such abundant sorrow and perplexity'. Confessing to weeping while writing, he lamented how 'the angry Angel of God visited my house with the plague'.

He knew he was not the only Londoner suffering. His enemy George Wharton was not expected to live: he had contracted the plague in mid-August and his condition was worsening. Elias Ashmole was severely unwell too: since the end of June he had had a series of agues and fevers which he had been unable to recover from.

Suddenly, the silence in the Corner House was broken by the sound of a knock at the door. Startled, Lilly opened it to discover a tall, round-faced, pox-marked and red-haired gentlewoman standing on his doorstep. When she asked to come in, he refused, explaining that he had 'buried a maid-servant of the plague very recently'. 'I fear not the plague, but the pox,' she said; at this he let her in.

His customer was Madame Jane Whorewood, a confidante of Charles I's, who as an intelligencer or agent was involved in smuggling funds and information across the country in support of the royalist cause. The King was planning to escape from Hampton Court, Whorewood told Lilly: he was fearful the soldiery were planning an assassination attempt and wanted to remove himself from the army's clutches.

His preference, she went on to explain, was to go into hiding somewhere close to London. This was because he hoped to take advantage of the situation in the agitated metropolis, where the citizens were 'alienated in affection from the Parliament, inclining wholly to his Majesty, and very averse to the army'. Could Lilly give judgement on the query, 'In what quarter of this nation he might be most safe, and not to be discovered until he himself pleased?'

Lilly set to work erecting a figure. It did not take him long.

Within half an hour, he judged Charles should flee 'about twenty miles (or thereabouts) from London'. The county of Essex, he advised Whorewood, was the best place for the monarch to 'continue undiscovered'.

Whorewood, who was known for her sharp intellect, thought quickly and 'remember'd a place in Essex about that distance, where was an excellent house, and all conveniences for his reception'. Pleased, she thanked Lilly and left, promising him twenty pieces of gold for his counsel.

Closing the door behind her, Lilly shook his head. He hoped his King would take his advice but feared he may not, since the monarch had many proffering him help; at least he had done what he could. But now he had to return to his manuscript: the deadline was more pressing than ever.

He had elected an auspicious time for printing *Christian Astrology* – choosing the moment when the Midheaven (*Medium Coeli* or MC) of his nativity, the point signifying his career and status, was directed to the terms of Mercury, planet of writing and communication, in the fixed zodiac sign of kingly Leo. He did not want to miss this opportune moment to confer lasting honours on his book.

The question was, could he complete it before another in his household fell victim to the plague? Would he even survive? Or would his democratic, astrology-for-all instruction manual be his final publication?

Chapter 3

The Intelligencer of the Stars

Mercury signifies intellect, communication, reason and wit,
the trickster, learning, the magician and youth.
It is associated with quicksilver, hermaphrodites and the hyaena,
dissembling, markets, merchants, the mind and the hands.

The cannoneer turned quickly, putting his prospective-glass down and shouting to his men and Lilly, to whom he had just been talking: 'Look to yourselves, the cannon in the castle is about to be discharged.' Hastily, Lilly and the New Model Army gunners ran for cover under an old ash tree; seconds later the cannon-bullet came hissing over them and, thankfully, missed. 'No danger now,' said one of the gunners, 'but', he urged William, 'begone for there are five more charging.'

While the King's men worked through the laborious process of priming and loading the cannons on the besieged Colchester castle, Lilly took his opportunity and left. He was lucky. Two hours later, the cannoneer he had been conversing with and another soldier were killed when the castle cannons fired their next round at the parliamentary forces surrounding the town. When he visited the soldiery again the following morning, he 'saw the blood of the two poor men lie upon the planks'.

It was mid-July 1648 – the peak of what would become known as the second Civil War. Lilly and John Booker had been called to the battle front to encourage and assure Parliament's army that the royalist forces, who had been holding Colchester for over a month, would surrender soon.

Both sides were suffering heavy bombardment. Since the astrologers had arrived, the steeple of St Mary's church, where the royalists had sited a very large cannon, had been badly battered and damaged by cannon fire. With food running out and water spoiled or cut off, the town's inhabitants were increasingly desperate. Even so, the cavalier commanders, the Earl of Norwich and Sir Charles Lucas, were holding out in the hope that military action around the country would go their way.

Inside the city wall, Sir Lucas (whom Lilly knew well) was also taking astrological direction. His star-gazer, John Humphreys, had briefly been a pupil of Lilly's at the start of the decade, but the two men were never friends: William found Humphreys foolhardy, loquacious and vainglorious; Humphreys had recently published a pamphlet, *Anti-Merlinus,* attacking his former tutor.

Now Humphreys was prolonging the misery of the siege by deluding Lucas with expectation of imminent relief. This was false intelligence (Humphreys would later have his feet whipped – the bastinado – and be thrown into prison for this deception). Royalist risings scattered across the country were abortive or had been suppressed, and the only relief on the horizon was a long way off – the Scots, currently fighting for the King, had crossed the border and were marching south against Cromwell.

Lilly said that if he could have obtained leave to enter the fortress town to give Lucas his view of 'the condition of affairs as they then stood', he would have done so. This did not happen. So, after two days, having encouraged Parliament's troops (led by General Thomas

Fairfax) as much as they could and having been 'well entertained at the headquarters', Lilly and Booker were returning to London.

The two men were firm friends with much in common, personally and professionally, and plenty to compare and discuss as they headed back to the metropolis. They were of similar ages, Booker the senior by just a month, and both had been bright lads who were denied university educations. They were the vanguard of the new generation of astrologers who were not university-educated.

Booker was a country boy too: born in Manchester in the county of Lancashire, he had headed to London to serve an apprenticeship to a haberdasher in Laurence Lane. Dissatisfied, he left for employment as a writing master at Hadley School in Middlesex, and was later clerk to city justice of the peace Sir Christopher Clethero and alderman Sir Hugh Hammersley prior to establishing his astrological practice.

When Lilly arrived in the city, he had worked as a manservant to Gilbert Wright, the master of the Company of Salters (one of London's twelve great livery companies), and his first wife, Margery. Wright was illiterate and he wanted a youth who could write to attend to him and his wife (walking in front of him on his way to church and accompanying him when he travelled).

In addition, there were 'all manner of drudgeries' for William to carry out: cleaning shoes, sweeping the house and the street, making fires, weeding the garden, scraping trenchers (the wooden boards that food was cut and served on), fetching beer and bundles of firewood when his master and mistress had lodgers, and lugging tubs of water from the river Thames. He worked in service at the Corner House for over six years.

William's introduction to astrology came during these first years in the capital. Margery, who was in a loveless second marriage and was lonely, enthralled him with tales of her visits to Simon Forman's consulting rooms. He yearned to be able to study the art himself, but did not have the resources to do so. It was another eleven years before he began his study with John Evans.

During that time, Margery died of the breast cancer that Lilly helped treat and Gilbert Wright married again to a wealthy widow, Ellen Whitehaire, but passed away not long after. Lilly's new mistress had by then been married twice to older men and widowed twice, and she had had enough. This time, she desired a young fellow and it was 27-year-old William she set her sights on. Their clandestine wedding made him a man of means and leisure – and gave him the opportunity to devote himself to astrology.

Booker had become interested in foretelling the future much earlier. Like Lilly, he excelled at Latin as a youth, and as soon as he was able to understand the star science, he dedicated himself to it; William thought he had 'seemed from his infancy to be designed for astrology'. With his head start, Booker set up his astrological rooms a few years ahead of his friend and began publishing almanacs in 1631 – more than a decade before Lilly.

Booker was the first to taste fame too. In his 1632 pamphlet *A New Almanac and Prognostication*, he forecast that solar eclipses due on 3 October 1632 and 29 March 1633 augured the death of royalty and the fall of kingdoms. A month after the first eclipse, the mighty King Gustavus Adolphus of Sweden was killed in battle and then four days later Frederick King of Bohemia died – both had been major players in the Thirty Years' War which was shedding blood across Continental Europe.

Lilly was among those impressed by Booker's prescience: for a time, he considered John 'the greatest and most complete astrologer in the world'. His colleague went from strength to strength: his almanacs were bestsellers (the edition for 1640 had a print run of 12,000) and his consulting rooms were continually busy. Now the friends, united in their love for the mantic art, were at the peak of their profession and revelling in the challenges it was bringing.

It was not the first time they had worked together in Parliament's service. Months earlier, the two friends were taken by coach and horses to the army's then headquarters at Windsor to help resolve differences between the New Model Army and the now Independent-led Parliament (following the New Model's purge of Presbyterian MPs at the end of 1647).

There, the men reassured both the soldiery and General Fairfax that God was on their side and that together Parliament and its army would conquer and subvert its enemies, winning 'a quiet settlement and firm peace over all the nation'. In their meeting, General Fairfax admitted to them that he did not understand the celestial science, but 'hoped it was lawful and agreeable to God's word'.

They also took the opportunity to visit their friend, army chaplain Hugh Peter, who was lodging at Windsor Castle. Peter, an Independent minister, was known for his rousing pre-battle sermons for the New Model Army and his success in converting surrendered cavalier soldiers to the parliamentary cause. The three men had much to mull over, including the latest slights at Lilly and Peter in a recent royalist pamphlet. 'Listen to this,' Peter declared, reading aloud:

> From the oracles of the sibyls so silly,
> The curst predictions of William Lilly,
> And Dr. Sybbald's Shoe-Lane philly,
> Good Lord, deliver me.

Laughing at the memory of that meeting, Lilly and Booker reminisced some more. Both were now used to the insults dealt out in print and song. Booker was himself the subject of the most famous cavalier ballad of all – 'When the King enjoys his own again' – sung to raise royalist spirits. They knew the verse and melody well; the ballad began:

> What Booker doth prognosticate
> Concerning Kings' or kingdoms' fate?
> I think myself to be as wise
> As some that gazeth on the skies;
> My skill goes beyond the depth of a pond,
> Or rivers in the greatest rain,
> Thereby I can tell all things will be well
> When the King enjoys his own again.

The men fell silent as they approached London. Lilly's thoughts turned to what he could not divulge to Booker, or anyone else. It was not just Parliament who wanted his help: the tense months preceding the renewal of fighting in late spring 1648 had seen all the major players coming to him for assistance.

The King, who had not taken Lilly's advice the previous year to escape from Hampton Court to Essex, but had instead fled south and been captured, had, despite this, sent word to him once more in March. At this point, Charles was incarcerated in Carisbrooke Castle on the Isle of Wight but was keen to take advantage of recent royalist uprisings in Kent, the continued readiness of London's citizens to revolt against Parliament and the alliance he had recently forged with the Scots. To that end, Jane Whorewood had visited Lilly again to apprise him of the sovereign's latest escape strategy.

The plan, Whorewood told Lilly, was for the King to escape by sawing through the iron bars of his chamber window. A small ship, anchored not far from the castle, would then take him to Sussex. Horses there were ready to carry him through the county into Kent 'so that he might be at the head of the army in Kent, and from thence to march immediately to London, where thousands then would have armed for him'.

This time, Lilly's part in the scheme was practical. Could he obtain a saw to cut the iron bars and an amount of the alchemical liquid *aqua fortis* (nitric acid)? William had provided both: the King had cut the bars of his window, but then he had got stuck on the way out and the plot was foiled. After that, the King was watched more closely and further opportunities to flee did not come about.

Another client whom Lilly was keeping quiet about was Richard Overton. He sought his advice just over a month after Whorewood's second visit. However, as he was unable to see William in person, he had instead written his query down and sent it to the Corner House.

This method of consulting was not unusual. Many clients could not travel to the city; others approached him for the first time at the Corner House and afterwards communicated by letter. Since Lilly had recently invited his readers to write to him, either with their questions or with observations of unusual celestial occurrences in their locale, correspondence to the Corner House was on the increase.

Some, like Overton, employed a messenger to send their query. The majority posted their problems to him, courtesy of the recently introduced postal service, the Royal Post. This was opened up to the public in 1635 by Charles I; prior to this it was for royal mail only. War had made the service more haphazard, but as Lilly's mailbag showed, post did reach its destination.

William's technique for answering queries on paper was exactly the same as for answering them in person – he noted the time he understood the question. With a face-to-face consultation this was when he heard the query; with a written request it was when he read it.

In Overton's case, he opened the small, 6cm by 7cm, scrap of paper and read the question on it on Saturday, April 29 at 12.45pm, so that was the time he used to draw up the relevant horary chart (CHART 3, BELOW).

The Leveller leader had written: 'Whether by joining with the agents of the private soldiery of the army for the redemption of commonright and freedom to the land and removal of oppression from the people my endeavours shall be prosperous or no. Richard Overton.'

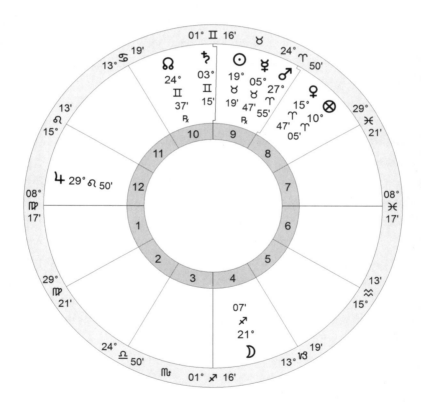

CHART 3 Richard Overton's horary chart (based on Lilly's original chart for 29 April 1648)

He asked this on the very eve of the second Civil War. The Scottish Parliament was days away from ordering the raising of an army against the parliamentarians, and Englishmen wishing to join the royalist fight were heading north. News of this Scottish mobilization had just reached Westminster and the army in Windsor, and MPs had responded by suspending their policy not to negotiate any further settlement terms with the King. Meanwhile, the New Model Army was poised to move against the continuing royalist uprisings in Kent.

In addition to this manoeuvring, Overton's question was potentially triggered by a decision on 24 April by leaders within the army to resume their demands for political reform. At the end of the previous year, the Levellers had contributed to the army's debates about its blueprint for a new political system (although the radicals were disappointed ultimately about the extent to which their demands were incorporated within the army's). Now, here was another opportunity to wield influence.

In Overton's horary figure of heaven, his chief significator (the planet ruling the sign on the Ascendant) was Mercury, planet of communication, intellect and writing – particularly apt for a prolific, witty pamphleteer. However, the poor condition of Mercury in the chart gave cause for concern. Its position was too close to the Sun, a situation known as 'being under the sunbeams', signifying that Overton was somehow in a poor condition – potentially not in the best of health, or suffering from a lack of confidence – perhaps because two other key Levellers, John Lilburne and John Wildman, were then imprisoned.

Mercury was also retrograde (meaning that from the point of view of an observer on Earth it appeared to be moving backwards in the sky). In astrological theory, this was not a good omen. It was the sign of someone who could well change their mind about the matter in hand, or someone who was revisiting a situation or going over old ground.

The chart was worrying in other ways too. Overton's co-significator, the Moon, was in freedom-loving Sagittarius in the fourth house of the land, but it was adjacent to the *Cauda Draconis*, the Dragon's Tail, a point of misfortune – another augury of trouble.

Despite all this, the horary revealed that Overton and the army – signified by Mars in Aries – would work together in the future. The Moon was applying by a beneficial trine aspect to Mars: horary's rules of timing suggested this would happen in just under seven months' time (as the Moon was just short of seven degrees away from an exact trine aspect with Mars). Overton and the Levellers should expect to be able to influence the army in November that year.

There was a final warning, though. The end of the matter in horary is signified by the planet ruling the zodiac sign on the cusp of the fourth house. This was Jupiter, but unfortunately it was in the maleficent twelfth house, the house of secret enemies, self-sacrifice and imprisonment. Overton's chart described the Levellers working with the New Model Army but not enjoying the outcome they hoped for.

Arriving in London, Lilly bade Booker farewell. The two men were equal in many parts, but not when it came to family and married life. Booker was looking forward to seeing his wife and four children (two girls and two boys), one of whom, Victoria, had been so christened in 1644 in anticipation of Parliament's eventual victory.

In contrast, William and his spouse Jane remained childless and his heart was heavy at the thought of her: to his mind, Jane was 'of the nature of Mars'. It was work, as usual, that was on his mind.

* * * *

Bidding him thank you and adieu, the striking, red-haired gentlewoman once again closed the door of the Corner House. This time Jane Whorewood had, with the King's consent, visited Lilly to ask him to elect the most auspicious time for Charles I to speak with parliamentary commissioners about a possible peace settlement.

It was now mid-September 1648 and the nation was in ferment about what was to happen to its monarch. Charles had lost the second Civil War: Colchester had surrendered in late August – after hearing that Cromwell's men had defeated the Scots at the Battle of Preston, and Fairfax had then taken the controversial decision to execute the royalist commanders, the Earl of Norwich and Sir Charles Lucas.

However, like the first military victory, the fighting did not solve anything politically. The alliance between Parliament and the New Model Army had won the battles, but the two groups were divided about the nature of a settlement with the King. In Parliament, the Presbyterians had regained the upper hand when army officers had left to crush the earlier royalist uprising. They were now using this majority to reopen negotiations with the King, a decision that left many within the army deeply unhappy.

The militant position was that all deals with the sovereign should be halted. Charles I had blood on his hands. He had led the country back into war and was not to be trusted: all discussions so far with him had been mired in duplicity and game-playing. Across the land, these militants were mobilizing petitions arguing against treaties.

In addition, the Levellers were making their presence felt. They had secured John Lilburne's release from the Tower of London at the start of August and reopened contact with Cromwell and the Independents. Then on 11 September they published and presented to Parliament *The Humble Petition of Thousands of Well-Affected Persons*. In the petition, they condemned a settlement by personal treaty with Charles, describing his notorious 'underhand dealing', and called for a deal providing justice for those involved in the wars and guaranteeing religious toleration.

Two days later, the presentation to MPs at the House of

Commons of a second petition repeating the demands of the first caused uproar. The leading royalist newsbook *Mercurius Pragmaticus* reported that during the disturbance, junior army officers were heard saying to members that 'they knew no use of a King or Lords any longer; and that such distinctions were the devices of men, God having made all alike'.

The result was a nation in turmoil, facing a multitude of unknowns. Would the King agree to the settlement that parliamentary commissioners were now preparing, and would such a deal back Presbyterianism and deny religious toleration? Would Charles try to escape again? Was he trying to forge a third Civil War, this time with Irish and Continental help?

In addition, would the Levellers persuade the army to oppose any personal settlement with the monarch? What exactly did their call for 'justice' mean? Was it, as *Mercurius Pragmaticus* suggested, a demand that 'the King may be called to account in a criminal way'?

At Whorehood's request, Lilly had done what he could to elect a time for Charles Stuart, but it had not been straightforward. Elections – selecting the optimum moment for a venture – were one of the most complex astrological techniques and required considerable time, as well as sidereal skill, to carry out optimally.

Not only did the astrologer have to locate a point in time when planetary positions symbolized the desired outcome or priorities, but also the particular instant chosen must align favourably with the birth chart of the individual requesting the election. In addition, the key planets in the election should be, astrologically speaking, in a good condition (meaning that they could exert their full influence). With so many criteria to meet, the perfect election chart did not exist.

For example, when the city of Baghdad was founded in 762 CE, the time that was chosen by the team of court magi for the first stone to be laid had to both signify the immediate and long-term aims for the metropolis, as well as honour the natal chart of Caliph Abu Jafar al-Mansur.

The election chart for this moment – 2.40pm local time on 31 July 762 (New Style (NS) Gregorian calendar) (CHART 4, BELOW) – suggests that the priorities for the new capital of the Islamic empire were power, prosperity and pleasing the chief. However, the horoscope also indicates that peace was not a top priority for Baghdad.

The astrologers found a moment when the Sun, signifying the caliph, and the great benefic Jupiter were in strong positions – this

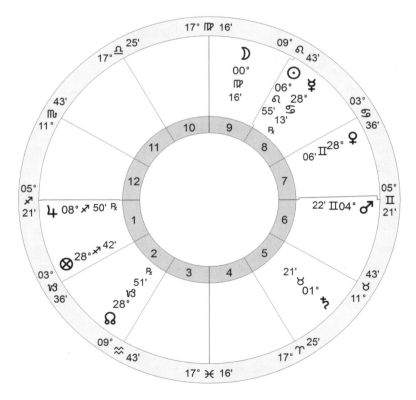

CHART 4 The election chart for the city of Baghdad. 31 July 762 (NS)

conveyed longevity, greatness and success. The Sun was in Leo, the zodiac sign it rules, where it is said to be dignified, and was in the ninth house of learning (the house of its joy), and close to the royal star Regulus.

Jupiter, the planet of wisdom and wealth, blazed with strength, brilliance and staying power: it was conjunct the Ascendant and dignified in its own sign of Sagittarius, and as Sagittarius was the sign on the Ascendant, Jupiter was Baghdad's signifier. Jupiter also ruled the fourth house of foundations, and was in a favourable trine aspect to the Sun in the ninth house – auguring Baghdad's role as a seat of learning. So far, so good.

But directly across from Jupiter in the chart, the malefic, martial planet Mars was placed ominously in the seventh house of open enemies – signifying that peace would be in short supply. The city could expect conflict and attack to be a common occurrence.

Fortunately for Baghdad, there was an ameliorating factor. Mercury was the planet signifying the metropolis's enemies (it is the lord of the seventh house – the planet ruling the sign Gemini at the start of this house). However, Mercury was in a severely debilitated position: it was retrograde; in the eighth house of death; conjunct the Tail of the Dragon and combust under the Sun's close rays. With Mercury in such a poor condition, the city's many enemies throughout the years would be unlikely to have the upper hand. Overall, the election time proved acceptable for the caliph's astrologers.

Typically, an astrologer could spend many hours searching for the best possible moment, often looking weeks, months or years ahead. Lilly did not have this luxury in electing Charles's auspicious moment: the commissioners were drawing up their propositions and preparing to visit the sovereign (who was still being held on the Isle of Wight). Whorewood needed an answer that morning regarding an immediate date and time; he did his best.

One aim in elections was to strengthen the ruler of the individual's Ascendant. In Charles's case this was the Sun, as his Ascendant was in the regal sign of Leo. However, the Sun had just moved into Libra, the sign of its fall, and would be there for the next month. Lilly had to look for another way to bolster the Sun, such as placing it at its peak on the Midheaven on the cusp of the tenth house, by timing the talks to begin at midday (a move John Dee had used when fine-tuning the moment of Queen Elizabeth I's coronation).

There were possibilities. On Monday 18 September, just before midday, with the Sun strong on the Midheaven and close to a conjunction with benefic Venus dignified in Libra, the sign rising above the horizon was exactly conjunct the King's natal Sun. But as usual with elections, there would have to be compromises.

Eventually, Lilly 'elected a day and hour when to receive the commissioners and propositions'. He also advised Jane Whorewood that Charles should not delay: as soon as he read the propositions, he should sign them if there was to be any chance of a peaceful settlement. Satisfied with this, she had left.

Lilly's decision to help Charles Stuart again, despite his personal support for Parliament, was rooted in part in his stance that a bloodless settlement between the King and his people was the best way forward for the nation. '*Anglicus* is yet for monarchy, as most consonant to English constitutions ... I desire his Majesty should be restored,' remained his view.

But there was another reason for his mercurial actions. He had been a practising astrologer for fifteen years, and part of his code of ethics was to be 'familiar to all'. He was God's conduit; it was his role to judge charts, not souls.

Lilly explained the principles he attempted to work and live by at the start of *Christian Astrology*. This one-page address 'To the student in astrology' was in essence an astrological Hippocratic oath: it was a mix of both professional and personal advice, and clearly underlined his belief that divination was a religious act:

> The more holy thou art; and more near to God, the purer judgement thou shalt give. Beware of pride and self-conceit ... As thou daily conversest with the heavens, so instruct and form thy mind according to the image of divinity; learn all the ornaments of virtue, be sufficiently instructed therein; be humane, courteous, familiar to all, easy of access, afflict not the miserable with terror of a harsh judgement; in such cases, let them know their hard fate by degrees; direct them to call on God to divert his judgements impending over them: be modest, conversant with the learned, civil, sober man, covet not an estate; give freely to the poor, both money and judgement: let no worldly wealth procure an erroneous judgement from thee, or such as may dishonour the art, or this divine science:
>
> Love good men, cherish those honest men that cordially study this art: Be sparing in judgement against the common-wealth thou livest in. Give not judgement of the death of thy Prince; yet I know experimentally, that *Reges subjacent legibus stellarum* ['Kings are subject to stellar laws'], marry a wife of thy own, rejoice in the number of thy friends, avoid law and controversy:
>
> In thy study, be all that you can be so that you may be singular in skill; be not extravagant or desirous to learn every science, be not a jack of all trades; be faithful, tenacious, betray no one's secrets, no, no I charge thee never divulge either friend or enemies trust committed to thy faith.
>
> Instruct all men to live well, be a good example thyself, avoid the fashion of the times, love thy own native country:

exprobrate no man, no not an enemy: be not dismayed, if ill spoken of, *Conscientia mille testes* ['Conscience is a thousand witnesses']; God suffers no sin unpunished, no lie unrevenged.

This guidance was proving popular. His book was selling well: so well indeed that he would be giving his first public talk before the end of the year. In fact, all aspects of his business were prosperous. Sales of his pamphlets were up year on year: in 1646, he had sold 13,500 copies, last year 17,000, and this year figures so far were higher – approaching 18,500. Because his publications were bestsellers, he could now command the top rate for a pamphleteer – £70 per annum, whereas the less well-known writers were paid an annual fee of between £2 to £15, depending on experience.

The extent of his renown and influence could be seen in the decision by several newsbooks that year to reprint his monthly astrological reports as 'circulation-builders'. Other publishers simply lifted his prophecies and reprinted them without permission in their own compilations. Dubbed 'the intelligencer of the stars', he was the nascent newspaper industry's first publishing celebrity.

In his consulting rooms he was seeing upwards of 1,000 clients annually. His rates varied, according to the customer's circumstances. The poor received free counsel, while the usual fee was between a shilling and a half-crown (2 shillings and 6 pence) – a shilling was about a day's wages for a labourer; half a crown the cost of a wine glass produced domestically; 3d (pence) the price of a modest tavern meal. (In comparison, the less well-known astrologer, John Vaux, charged one shilling.)

Tutoring was another source of finance. He had mentored some students since his early days in the profession and then, two years ago, he had advertised his services, announcing in *Anglicus* 'if any that are studious require satisfaction in this art, I live at …' In *Christian Astrology* he claimed he had 'made more scholars in this profession, than all that profess this art in England'.

Prices for tuition varied too. Back in the 1630s, John Humphreys had paid £40 to spend three days out of seven with him for a period of six weeks. This was a particularly handsome sum, considering that a shopkeeper's salary was around £45 per annum and a newsbook editor's weekly salary £3. The charge was extortionate because he did not like Humphreys. Ever mindful of the type of astrologer he was creating, he later refused to reveal to Humphreys all he knew, especially his occult knowledge, despite Humphreys's pleadings to pay £200 if he would.

However, he did agree to teach him the trick that was guaranteed to amaze every client – pinpointing a client's secret moles and hidden birthmarks when analyzing their horary chart. This was done by considering the sign on the Ascendant at the start of the first house, as well as the sign on the cusp of the sixth house of sickness and its planetary ruler.

In recent months, his income had been given another boost when he started to receive a state pension of £100 per annum, in addition to a one-off lump sum of £50. This was for his intelligence-gathering work: he had been asked by Parliament to use his extensive contacts in Continental Europe to get key information out of France; he was also 'familiar with all the spies that constantly went in and out of Oxford' and knew all the places the spy network used to pass on messages.

All of these revenue streams, plus the sum of nearly £1,000 (approaching £80,000 today) he inherited after the death of his first wife and the property investments he made with it (a half share in twelve London houses in the Strand, including the Corner House), meant that he was a gentleman of competent fortune by 1648.

Now, with his first talk imminent, he was poised to expand his trade and public profile. More presentations were planned for next year. His aim of educating and opening up the profession was becoming a reality.

* * * *

It was late in the day on 4 December 1648, and Lilly was close to completing next year's almanac. This edition was different in a number of ways. There was a new title, *Merlinus Anglici Ephemeris*, and a new front cover showing a woodcut engraving of himself holding a horoscope inscribed with his motto *Non cogunt* – 'They do not compel' (this was the first time an almanac had included an author's portrait). Moreover, inside he had addressed his readers for the first time as 'the commonalty of England'.

The differences also included his emotions while writing – this *Anglicus* had been written with a 'mournful quill'. What he had hoped would not happen, had: instead of a peace settlement to restore Charles to his throne, a cascade of events had begun that were set to change England and its people forever. The King had not followed his directions: he had instead dragged the settlement negotiations out over days and weeks, and then after the 40-day-deadline was reached, an extension had been granted. But many within the army had had enough of the monarch's delaying tactics.

Commissary-general Henry Ireton, an Independent MP and Cromwell's son-in-law, took action. After drafting *The Remonstrance of the Army*, which called for an end to a treaty with Charles and for the sovereign to be put on trial, he presented it to the Council of the Army on 10 November; army leader Fairfax refused to support it.

Then, as Charles plotted another escape attempt, Cromwell and Ireton turned to the Levellers for support. Just as Overton's horary showed, during November the army and the Levellers worked together. On 20 November, a revised *Remonstrance*, representing the aims of both radicals and soldiers, was presented to the House of Commons; but Parliament's reaction was to delay debating it until December, and to grant the King another extension.

In response, the New Model Army and the radicals made their move. Throughout November, the army had been gathering close to London. Three days ago, on 1 December, the soldiers began to march towards the city and Charles was moved from the Isle of Wight to the mainland. The following day, the army made its headquarters in Whitehall Palace.

Now, on 4 December, Lilly and his fellow citizens had earlier in the day heard the news that the King had been seized; the anxious, army-occupied metropolis currently waited as the House of Commons debated what to do next. Was a deal with Charles still possible or would the army bring the King 'that man of blood, to account for the blood he had shed'?

In his almanac's opening words, Lilly addressed these concerns directly and made two predictions: a treaty with the King would not materialize and Parliament would be purged again. Regarding a settlement, he reminded his audience of the first four attempts to reach an agreement with Charles, and forecast: 'A fifth treaty, or propositions to be sent the fifth time, I fear no mortal man shall ever see'.

On the topic of Parliament's fate, he wrote: 'I may say of the members of this Parliament, as God said of Gideon's soldiers, You are too many, God will be glorified and act his decrees by means of a few upright spirits amongst them … God hath spewed bishops quite out of England, let his first born son Presbyter expect the next purge, if he continue tyrannical as he begins.'

Today he intended to conclude his almanac by informing the nation of his belief that the King's destiny was book-ended by the appearance of two eclipses. The first was a solar eclipse that had occurred nearly a decade before at the end of May 1639 when Charles's eleven years of 'personal rule' (governing without recourse to Parliament) was coming to an end, and Parliament and people were growing restless. The second was a lunar eclipse that had taken place just days earlier on Charles's birthday.

Eclipses had always been read as signifying great change to rulers: the majority of early omen astrology centred on eclipses of the luminaries and their implications for monarchy. An example from the 17th century BCE reads:

> On the 16th day an eclipse takes place,
> The king dies,
> And the marshes the streams irrigate.

However, it was also understood that eclipses did not signify an inevitable royal death. The ancient Babylonians believed, just as Lilly did millennia later, that the destinies traced out in the starry firmament were not binding ones. Fate could be loosened or relaxed by negotiating with, or propitiating, the deities – a belief outlined in the Babylonian incantation, 'Ea [the god of wisdom and cunning] has wrought it, Ea has loosed it.'

In ancient Mesopotamia, mollifying the divinities in order to protect a ruler from an eclipse took the form of prayers, rituals, purification rites, incantations and lamentations. It even included installing a substitute king and his consort on the throne and then killing the couple. (The period at the palace, during which the stand-ins were dressed in imperial robes and treated as royalty but watched over by court guards, could stretch for up to 100 days if it was felt that the danger augured by the eclipse lasted this long.)

Over the intervening millennia, belief in the power and

symbolism of eclipses did not wane (although the practice of slaughtering a commoner or criminal in order to protect the King was discontinued). Eclipses still caused considerable consternation in the 17th century, as the case of Pope Urban VIII and his astrological safe room to protect against eclipses showed, and astrologers continued to relate the appearance of eclipses to disturbances to the ruling elite (as Booker had done to great effect in 1632).

Lilly's fears for Charles's survival were triggered when he observed a number of worrying signs in the 1639 solar eclipse chart. Not only was the Moon eclipsing the Sun in the eighth house of death, but the eclipsed Sun, as the planetary ruler of Leo, was also the Lord of the tenth house (the house traditionally associated with kings). Even more ominously for the monarch, the eclipse in the house of death occurred opposite the position of Charles's Sun in his natal chart.

Nearly ten years ago, Lilly had judged: 'the Lord of the 10th is eclipsed. Sovereignty, regal power, majesty of long continuance, suffers obscuration … Sun is eclipsed by Moon: The commonalty grow heady, strong, violent, turbulent, impatient of former miseries wherein they lived … thraldom and mere necessity enforce the people to break out of bondage, and to eclipse their commanders'. He did not publish the manuscript in which he wrote these words.

Although the symbolism within the eclipse chart spoke to him of Charles Stuart's downfall, Lilly had remained true to his belief that the stars did not compel. If the King could be persuaded to change his course of action (by astrological counsel or another approach), then his fate could be altered. But stubborn Charles had stayed committed to his path.

For William, the lunar eclipse on the King's birthday five days ago had sounded the death knell. In his recent pamphlet, *Whether, or no, his Majesty shall suffer death*, he had written that 'the most material thing signified by this eclipse, is a strict questioning, and bringing to severe punishment' which would 'principally be effected in London and Westminster'.

Now, manuscript in front of him, he began cautiously to add more detail about whose fate was tied to this eclipse and when its effects would come to pass. 'I pass by many things concerning his Majesty,' he wrote, 'both with a tender hand and a mournful quill, being my self naturally an earnest lover of monarchy, nor am I willing to enlarge much against him ...'

However, he added, 'the eclipses of this year', in particular 'the most forciblest of all, viz. that of the 19 November, 1648 now operating, and all the revolutions [annual horoscopes], speak of very high things, and such as no age can parallel. The work of the day itself when it comes will be sufficiently sorrowful.'

To clarify that this was an individual of stature he was talking about, he stressed that 'the stern influence' of 'the eclipse in November 1648' would show itself 'not upon the meanest shrubs, but the tallest of all the English cedars, even upon such as may show a catalogue of many honourable or kingly ancestors'.

On timing, he forecast: 'these times will manifest, viz. in January 1649 there being a platick [perfect] trine betwixt Jupiter and Saturn; we may have strong hopes of being quite cured of our distempers ... we begin to smile; but monarchy is not in so great request as formerly'.

In the January section of the almanac's customary month-by-month forecasts, he wrote: 'I am serious, I beg and expect justice. The lofty cedars divine a thundering hurricane is at hand; many of the puny diminutive cedars cry welladay, their kingdom also is declining. The abused soldiery are inforced to be angry. O that *Anglicus* might be a true prophet.'

It would have to be enough. These were tense, bloodthirsty times: any more could earn him that cell in Newgate or worse. It was time to go to the printers. On the way, he would hopefully find out how matters were progressing in the House of Commons. The debate about whether to continue to negotiate with Charles had been going on all day; had an agreement been reached yet?

* * * *

After midday on Saturday 20 January 1649, Lilly went to Westminster to meet and talk with friends. This was not unusual for him – at this period he went there every Saturday afternoon. However, this was not a day like any other.

A peace settlement with Charles had not been reached. Instead, on 6 December, after Parliament had voted to try to negotiate further with the King, the army had purged Parliament of those MPs who supported such a treaty. Five weeks later, the severely reduced House of Commons, made up of members willing to put the monarch on trial for his life, set up a High Court of Justice which passed legislation enabling this. The nation was waiting for the trial to begin.

At Westminster, Lilly bumped into Hugh Peter. He had last seen the minister in mid-December, during the Christmas holidays. Then, Peter and Lord Grey of Groby (who had played a leading role in the purging of Parliament) had summonsed him to visit them at Somerset House – and to bring his latest pamphlets with him. They wanted to check what he had written regarding what was to happen in January.

On reading his January observations, Peter and Lord Groby appeared satisfied with his forecast. 'If we are not fools and knaves, we shall do justice,' Groby commented. Then, the two men whispered together, excluding Lilly from the rest of their conversation.

Now, on this January day at Westminster, Peter said to William, 'Come, Lilly, wilt thou go hear the king tried?' 'When?' said Lilly.

'Now, just now; go with me,' replied Peter, taking him by the arm and leading him up to the King's Bench in the Great Hall of Westminster, where they sat and waited for the trial to commence.

After fifteen minutes the judges arrived, and shortly after that the King came in dressed in the garb of a Knight of the Garter. Throughout the hearing, England's reigning monarch remained regal and dignified in his demeanour. He did not doff his hat to the officers of the court; he declined to recognize the legitimacy of the proceedings; he laughed at the charge of treason, and refused to plead his case.

When Lilly 'saw the silver top of his staff unexpectedly fall to the ground', Charles, King to the last, waited for another to pick it up. William thought his sovereign 'spoke excellently well, and majestically, without impediment in the least'.

John Bradshaw, the judge leading the court, eventually became provoked by the King's refusal to enter a plea and challenged Charles, saying: 'Sir, instead of answering the court, you interrogate their power, which becomes not one of your condition.' Hearing this, Lilly had had enough; in his heart he felt it was wrong 'to hear a subject thus audaciously to reprehend his sovereign'. He did not attend the remaining days of the trial.

On 25 January, Charles I was found to be guilty of treason; two days later he was condemned to death. He was executed by beheading on 30 January 1649 on a scaffold stage outside the Banqueting House at Whitehall Palace.

After the regicide, a rumour spread that Lilly had advised Parliament to make sure that Charles died by 30 January, since otherwise the stars suggested 'they should never have power to do it'. But Lilly denied any involvement in setting a date to kill the King.

However, he did admit that when a customer had asked him, 'If King Charles should be beheaded,' his response had been: 'I said, there would be much intercession for sparing of his life; and that if he escaped the last of January, it was possible he might live a little longer … But God determined his life to end the thirtieth of January.' Lilly suspected that his client, whom he did not identify, had gossiped; he did all he could to quash the rumour.

With the King dead, it was William's face that was the most famous in England. With his star in the ascendant, his goal was to see his profession develop in power and influence in the new Commonwealth of England he had helped to create.

However, he was aware of problems ahead. He had already hinted in one of his recent almanacs that whomever took up the reins of governing the republic would not be long in office. He was curious to see how the new polity was going to work out.

Chapter 4

'Ye Famous Mr William Lilly'

Venus signifies relationships, beauty and appearance,
luxury, art and the urge for cooperation and harmony.
It is associated with copper, the nightingale, figs and almonds,
myrtle, galleries, gardens, money and the kidneys.

It was a shock to see the young gentleman standing once more on the doorstep of the Corner House. Clad in a scarlet cloak wrapped tight to protect him from the chill air in late November 1649, and with a demicastor (a hat made of beaver fur) pulled down snug on his head, he looked harried and far more subdued than his usual ebullient self. Despite his surprise, Lilly had a suspicion about why the visitor was there and so, not saying a word, he simply turned and gestured him to step inside.

Once over the threshold, he bade the 32-year-old man take off his outer garments and sit down. Underneath the vermilion cape, the rest of his clothes were just as striking. He was dressed in a cloth suit trimmed with gold, a black Spanish leather belt and a Holland shirt embroidered with ☿ – the astrological glyph for the planet Mercury (which Lilly knew the young man considered to be the strongest planet in his nativity). On one hand was a black enamelled ring, in his

85

left ear a cornelian ring. William noted that his fine, wavy, light brown hair had thinned more at the temples, revealing the scar on the right-hand side of his forehead. He also still smelt faintly of the ointment he applied regularly to his scalp in the hope of his hair growing again.

An awkward silence enveloped the two men. Lilly let it linger. It had been nearly two years since he had spoken with the star-gazer in front of him – Elias Ashmole. Nearly two years since Ashmole had betrayed him publicly and broken off all contact.

The rift in their friendship had not been entirely unexpected. He had always suspected that Ashmole's loyalties were split – the young lawyer had already been close friends with George Wharton when they met. However, what he did not realize for a long time was that, throughout their relationship, Ashmole had been passing information to Wharton about Lilly and his clients. The older royalist had then used this to try to discredit him.

In November 1647, Wharton became editor of the latest cavalier newsbook, *Mercurius Elencticus*, and used his new position to increase his printed attacks on Lilly. *Elencticus* was a pedantic and dull read, and Wharton admitted in private that 'if he mentioned not Lilly in his Mercuries, they would not sell …'

In the issue for the week beginning 12 November, Wharton described his adversary as 'that juggling wizard William Lilly, the state's figure-flinger general, a fellow made up of nothing but mischief, tautologies and barbarism' and declared that he looked 'like a pig, over-roasted'. He then went on to claim that Lilly had used 'cheating tricks' and 'abominable practices' to enable a customer, Mr John Howe of Lincoln's Inn, to win the affections of, and marry, wealthy Lady Annabella Scroope, daughter of the Earl of Sunderland.

Lilly had advised Lady Annabella's suitor but strenuously denied any wrongdoing. However, he suspected immediately who Wharton's source of information was, and confronted Ashmole. At first, Elias hoped to persuade Lilly that he had not been the one to pass on the details of the case, but William was unconvinced. The betrayal stung. Ashmole had not only let him down personally, but had also sullied his professional reputation. Their amity ended.

However, William had played his own part in the souring of their friendship. Yes, he had been effusive in his public praise of Ashmole as a learned and loyal compatriot: his youthful associate, he wrote in *The World's Catastrophe* (1647), was 'my noble friend'; a 'worthy gentleman' endowed with a 'sharpness of wit' and 'well versed' in astrology.

But, by an act of omission, he had provided Ashmole with a reason to mistrust him. Ashmole had been curious about the details of Lilly's nativity, but William was not forthcoming. He had his reasons. Many astrologers chose to withhold some or all of the key planetary and horoscopic placements in their birth chart. This was because, in the hands of an opponent, the so-called five hylegiacal places – the positions of the Sun, Moon, Part of Fortune, Ascendant and Midheaven – could be used to determine an individual's time of death or their moments of weakness (as Lilly had done with Charles I).

William had even misled his public about his nativity. In his *Merlinus Anglicus Junior* for 1645, he wrote: 'In my nativity I have Venus in Taurus, in cazimi with the Sun; I have Mercury in Taurus and Mars in Virgo, two earthly signs, the reasons why my conceptions are so dull, and my speech and discourse so defective: I have Jupiter in Libra near *Spica Virginis*, and Saturn in Scorpio, the Moon in Pisces.'

Some of these placements were correct. He was happy to admit that Jupiter was adjacent to the fixed star *Spica Virginis* (CHART 5, PAGE 88). This was a fortunate placement: *Spica* is associated with success, renown and riches and when it is conjoined with Jupiter the forecast is for the individual to be popular, and enjoy social success and wealth.

However, Lilly had been economical with the truth and had not revealed four of the five hylegiacal places. He had been born in the early hours of a Saturday morning in his family's sizeable timber-framed thatched farmhouse on what was then May Day (11 May in today's Gregorian calendar).

This meant that, yes, his Sun was in Taurus, but he had lied about his Moon: it was not in Pisces, but in a far less favourable position – in Capricorn – the sign of its detriment. Giving incorrect information about where his Moon was, as well as omitting the astral

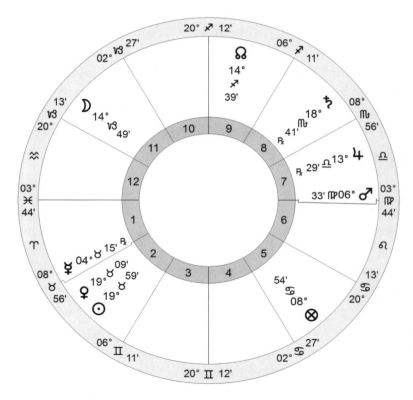

CHART 5 William Lilly's nativity, 1 May 1602

coordinates of his Ascendant, Midheaven and the Part of Fortune, meant there was no possibility that his audience or enemies could calculate his natal chart.

There was plenty to be circumspect about. His afflicted Moon in Capricorn spoke of gloominess and his tendency to melancholy. Malefic Saturn in intense Scorpio threw a dark shadow by opposition aspect to his Sun in steadfast Taurus, plus Saturn was in the eighth house of death and the black arts, suggesting he could be pulled towards these occult temptations.

His fifth house – the house of children – revealed that he would be unlikely to be a father. The house was empty, so the next planet to look to was that ruling the zodiac sign at the beginning of the house. This was the Moon (as Cancer was the sign on the cusp of the fifth house). However, the Moon was in a position where it was unable to operate effectively because it was in detriment in Capricorn – this signified a lack of fecundity.

Elsewhere in his birth chart there were ominous signs about the nature and number of his opponents. Mars and Jupiter were in the seventh house of relationships and open foes, and Saturn, the Lord of the twelfth house of secret enemies, was in a difficult opposition aspect to his Sun. These positions augured not just many foes, but ones who would express their malice openly and portended captivity or imprisonment. However, there was a ray of hope: Saturn was retrograde, denoting that William's opponents would be weaker than him and he could overcome them.

Venus's position revealed his financial good fortune. Benefic Venus, signifier of women, love and jewels, was in his second house – the house of riches, indicating that money would flow from Venusian sources: women, wedlock, love and dowries. For a man, this placement forecast the individual marrying his wife for her wealth.

Additional factors in his nativity corroborated and extended this forecast. Mars was in the seventh house of marriage and was the ruler of the eighth house (his wife's money) which denoted riches with a wife. However, malefic Mars's position also foresaw that the wife would die before the husband, and the wealth was not attainable without some scandal or trouble.

Lilly's first marriage to Ellen Whitehaire had been scandalous to many. When, after two years, the wedding of servant to mistress was revealed, there followed two further years of wrangling in the law courts to prevent the family of Ellen's first husband from taking her money. (Ellen had died twelve months after this verdict was secured and her full inheritance had passed to William.)

Now, as Lilly sat across from his former friend, he recalled hearing that Elias had remarried a few weeks earlier, after a lengthy search to find a rich wife. His new bride was apparently an older, wealthy widow. William was curious to hear the story – he had helped Ashmole at the start of his hunt for a suitable spouse. Breaking the silence, William enquired, 'How is married life?' All smiles, Elias responded enthusiastically. Then, pleasantries over, he revealed why he was there. He wanted Lilly to save George Wharton's life.

Wharton's troubles had begun in the spring of 1648 when the second Civil War had started. As Parliament moved to quell royalist uprisings around the country, it also moved to gag Wharton – the nation's loudest cavalier astrologer, who continued to incite the King's followers.

On 5 February 1648, the House of Commons Committee of the Militia discussed Wharton's pamphlet *No Merline nor Mercurie*, in which he attacked Parliament mercilessly. It then sent for him to be punished accordingly. The committee wanted to suppress such 'scandalous pamphlets' and 'to prevent the publishing and vending of the like for the future'.

Wharton was arrested just over a month later and sent to Newgate gaol, but escaped in September and went into hiding. He managed to evade recapture for over a year: during this time he continued to produce his pamphlets and, when he wanted, covertly arranged to meet his friends.

He fancied himself a poet and had recently sent Ashmole an invitation in verse to rendezvous with him at 7pm at the Three Tuns public house, near Clare Street. Fearful of being rearrested, he had signed himself George Lambert.

Waving this invitation at William, Elias read:

> My best of friends: If in these worst of times
> It lawful be to laugh in ought by rhymes:
> Pray let's enjoy some minutes of repose,
> And once more meet for to rejoice in prose.
> You know my constitution, it is such
> As cannot brook all airs: Nor yet too much
> Of any: and my genius so divine,
> It loves no liquor but a sprightly wine.
> If then you please to meet me where
> Maintain a friar never courts the nuns:
> At seven this evening, there expect your friend:
> Who (though he change his name) retained a mind
> Still honours you. His hand you (surely) know;
> And that's the cause he writes himself below.

But yesterday, Ashmole explained, Wharton had been discovered and taken to the Gatehouse prison in Westminster. This time Wharton was in serious trouble: the new republic was showing it was a force to be reckoned with by continuing to execute people who fought or conspired against it.

It did not help Wharton's cause that his new almanac for 1650 was as combative and colourful as ever. In it, he pledged to 'serve no mortal, but the cavalier'; railed against those who drenched their hands in the King's blood, accusing them of being not 'of the right English race' and 'degenerate so far from the true English nature'; denounced the current purged Parliament (which had signed Charles I's death warrant), protesting that its leaders were 'the most prodigious monsters that ever the earth groaned under'; and championed the future Charles II as 'monarch of my heart'.

John Bradshaw, who had presided over Charles I's trial and other trials of leading royalists, was the president of the Council of State (the Commonwealth's new executive body) and wanted the astrologer to hang. Ashmole pleaded with Lilly to use his many contacts within the Commonwealth's government to save Wharton from the scaffold.

Lilly did not hesitate. Expressing his sympathy at Wharton's situation and realizing immediately the gravity of the matter, he told Ashmole he would visit Bulstrode Whitelocke the next day. Whitelocke, he explained to him, would be chairman to the Council of State after Christmas; perhaps he could use his influence to obtain Wharton's release.

Lilly also promised to visit Wharton at the Gatehouse prison, to speak with as many of the other Council members as possible and to appear for Wharton at his hearing. He would do all he could, he reassured Ashmole.

Greatly relieved, Ashmole thanked William profusely for putting aside his quarrels with Wharton and with himself and for helping so generously. Lilly accepted his gratitude. Seeing the younger man to the door, he bade him farewell. He was happy to be of service: despite their many differences, he did not want Wharton to hang.

* * * *

Lilly shook his head and smiled ruefully as he turned from closing the door of the Corner House. It was Thursday 17 October 1650 and he had just spent an enjoyable morning with Elias Ashmole.

The two men had become firm friends again, since Lilly and his circle of allies had managed to secure George Wharton's release from jail in February of that year – on the proviso that Wharton 'would not thenceforward, writ against the Parliament or state'. In return, Ashmole had provided Lilly with legal advice, and Lilly had recently cemented their cordial relations by revealing the position of his natal Ascendant to him.

Elias was enjoying his new-found leisure and wealth: his wife Mary, Lady Manwaring had been left a jointure of £600 per annum (£48,000 today), and of this she had settled £200 per annum on Ashmole during her life. Casting horaries to answer his own queries filled a large portion of his days, as did his growing interest in alchemy and magic. He was also a regular visitor to his friend's home, bringing with him news and gossip and often a horary problem he wanted William to judge: should his friend Mrs Pordage sell her houses or keep them; who killed Roger Stevens's horse at Reading?

Today, the two men had discussed magic and two horaries, which were somewhat related. The first was: 'Whether it will be good for me to take the house near Boswell Court.' The newlyweds were currently staying with one of Ashmole's close friends, Dr Thomas Wharton (a physician of Trinity College, Oxford, and an astrology enthusiast), and were keen to find a marital home of their own; the address Elias had enquired about was in Carey Street, just a couple of minutes' walk from the Corner House.

Two considerations were uppermost in Ashmole's mind. The first was whether or not it was safe for him to remain in London. A month after Charles I's execution, the new Commonwealth had passed an Act of Parliament 'for removing all papists, officers, and delinquents

93

from London and Westminster, and confining them within five miles of their dwelling, etc'. The Act had been renewed on 19 March 1650.

Ashmole was right to be concerned for his liberty. During the early years of the war, he had been stationed with the King in Oxford; later he became a royalist Collector of Excise in Worcester. The fledgling Commonwealth had noted his cavalier allegiance and earlier in the year had recorded in its state papers: 'He is accounted a very dangerous man and is known to speak much against the Parliament. He doth make his abode in London notwithstanding the act of Parliament to the contrary.'

Elias's other primary consideration, as he explained delicately to Lilly, was whether or not the London house would be good for his wife's health. Almost 20 years older than her husband, Lady Manwaring had been married three times before and during one of these previous marriages had contracted a sexually transmitted infection, which she and Ashmole presumed to be 'a species of the pox'. Ashmole had been aware of her condition before the two agreed to wed, but since then had been growing more worried about his and his spouse's health.

Two days before his marriage, he consulted the stars as to 'whether ♄ [his astrological glyph for Mary in his diary] shall grow worse after she is marri[ed] in her disease or better'; two weeks after they wed, his wife requested he do a horary enquiring whether she had infected him with the pox. Some months later, when matters did not improve, he asked 'whether my wife shall live or die of this sickness ...' He wondered if the 'short-winded fits' she was experiencing were a consequence of the pox.

In a bid to protect himself and his bride, Ashmole had recently begun to craft sigils or talismans to ward off the disease. These magical charms (also known as lamins or telesmes) were typically worn as pendants or rings and were fashioned to embody the power of the planets and bestow this on their wearer. The maker drew the desired planet's potency down into the talisman by forging it with materials of cosmic sympathy: tin for Jupiter, gold for the Sun, iron for Mars, copper for Venus, silver for the Moon and lead for Saturn.

The particular planetary intensity embedded in the sigil could then be strengthened in a variety of manners: by engraving it with appropriate mantras, astrological glyphs or occult symbols; by invoking the blessings of specific angels; and by using the right suffumigations to dispel unwanted influences from the atmosphere (this involved burning aromatic woods like laurel, myrtle, rosemary and cypress).

Of the utmost importance, though, was timing all craftwork to take place at the most astrologically propitious moment possible. For example, to create a talisman to increase honour and reputation – qualities associated with Jupiter – the charm should be cast in tin and forged when Jupiter was in a favourable planetary position.

Lilly had given Ashmole the benefit of his experience in this realm. Nearly two decades ago, when he was exactly the same age as Elias was now, he had devoted many hours over a period of two years to the making of magical sigils. At the time, he was also teaching a Dutch physician John Hegenius how to use divining rods and craft talismans; and the result of their endeavours was a friendship and a collection of sigils that worked 'to very good purpose'.

He had enjoyed telling Elias about the first magical charm he ever set eyes on. Made of 'pure angel gold' (an angel was an old coin of high gold content) and 'of the bigness of a 33 shilling piece of King James coin', it had belonged to Margery, his first mistress at the Corner House, who kept it in a scarlet silk bag, together with her other sigils. This, she had told an enthralled teenage William, had been made by Simon Forman to protect her first husband from an evil spirit; it had saved his life.

The first sigils Ashmole experimented with were designed to drive various vermin – fleas, flies, caterpillars and toads – from the lodgings he and Lady Manwaring were then staying in. Using lead, Saturn's material, Elias cast them during a meeting in the heavens of Saturn and Mars (which occurred in July that year). He was very impressed with his charms, moulded in the actual shape of fleas, flies, caterpillars and toads, and had enjoyed telling his friends about their efficacy.

More recently, he had tried forging talismans of the nature of Venus and Mars to protect against the pox. This time, he experimented for nearly two weeks to see which configurations produced the greatest potency. Using periods of time when Scorpio, associated with the generative organs and their diseases, ascended over the horizon, he crafted a series of martial and venereal amulets – including some intricately fashioned in the shape of vaginas and penises.

The problem now, as he had today divulged to Lilly, was that Lady Manwaring could not find her pox talisman; she had been looking for it for three days and was growing increasingly anxious as to its whereabouts. Had she lost it, she wanted to know, or had she simply mislaid it? Casting a horary for 1.30pm, the men found the answer.

Astrological theory for finding lost things taught the astrologer to look to the position of the Moon and the planet ruling the zodiac sign the Moon was in. In this instance the sign was Sagittarius, whose ruler was Jupiter. The additional information needed to pinpoint the charm came from Jupiter's placement in watery, genital Scorpio. Ashmole had just hurried off home to take a look into his wife's chamber pot – the signs were that the sigil had dropped out and landed there while she was relieving herself.

With Ashmole gone, William moved to pick up the manuscript copy of his 1651 almanac. He had finished it yesterday and he had

YE FAMOUS MR WILLIAM LILLY

been about to head off to the printers with it when Elias had arrived. He would take it now: he was keen to see it in print.

The new Commonwealth had its hands full. It was governing still with a reduced number of members; was fighting campaigns against both the Irish and the Scots, was edging towards war with the Dutch, and was struggling to achieve a sense of legitimacy. Yet, in spite of all this, Lilly's judgement was that over the coming twelve months it would prevail against all opponents.

'The Commonwealth of England,' he predicted, 'cannot be destroyed or overcome by all the powers, and princes of Europe, were all their forces united in one body against it.' Its current strength, he explained, was revealed in the republic's charts for the year ahead. Here the stars showed 'the power of this present Parliament by sea or by land' to be 'essentially dignified, suffering no debilities either by position or aspect ...' and Mars was 'angular and in his exaltation'.

Considering this, he made an aggressive forecast aimed squarely at those factions looking to exploit any weaknesses in the new regime. 'This present power, authority, Parliament, Council of State, shall stand firm,' he wrote, 'and shall not be dissolved by any earthly power, worldly force, treachery, private divisions or imprecations of the priesthood whatsoever during this annual revolution. It's a bold assertion I maintain, for which the priest will lash me.'

Lilly was referring to the Presbyterians, who continued to preach against him and against astrology, and who were also highly dissatisfied with the present Parliament. Executing the King had not resolved England's quandary about how its religious communities should gather, and who should decide what was allowed in terms of belief and practice. The Presbyterians, thwarted in their desire to be the ones holding the reins of power, felt the situation was deteriorating rapidly.

In the ecclesiastical power vacuum, more radical sects were springing up and challenging the status quo and, to make matters worse, a year ago Parliament had shaken up the legal requirements regarding church attendance. The law requiring individuals to attend a service of the national church had been abolished; the act now in place still demanded attendance at a religious service but it was up to each individual to choose the type of service at which they wished to be present.

Lilly had baited the ministers, writing: 'When will the illiterate priest be quiet, or leave prating his seditious sermons to a fruitless auditory? Presbytery, thou shall not root in this kingdom.' He mocked their hopes to be 'made Lord Paramounts, judges or justices in all and every civil and temporal matter', and added, provocatively: 'who sees not their lewd practices to obtain it, hath neither eyes in his head or guts in his brains.'

Calling them 'stony-hearted pseudo-priests' and 'anti-parliamentarians', he had gone on the offensive, asking: 'How dare these men call themselves the sons of God or his ministers, since they act wholly for their own Mammon, and make it their whole labour to steal away the hearts of the people from their due obedience unto the Parliament … I fear not their bellowing or thundering against me or astrology, I seek God in his own words …'

He had also included incendiary forecasts for Cancerian countries – this meant Scotland and Holland, which both had their Ascendant in the zodiac sign of Cancer. Ill-omened Saturn had moved into Cancer and, in the Commonwealth's chart, it was in a tense square aspect with the Sun. To the Scottish people he predicted that by October next year they would suffer as much loss as was possible. To the Dutch he foretold that, in more than twelve months' time, the fullness of God's vengeance was waiting for them:

'I will speak such language unto the Hollander, as their ears who read it shall tingle … the living Dutch shall tremble, and scarce have a resting place in any port of east India or other country, so hateful shall their names be ... this shall assuredly come to pass though not in this year, let them expect what is said in Jer. [Jeremiah] 51. ver. 13. Oh thou that dwellest upon many waters, abundant in treasure, thine end is come, and the measure of thy covetousness ... We shall be victorious with our army at land and at sea.'

Overall, he thought, his almanac was sure to prompt discussion. Picking up his plain black cloak, he prepared to leave for the printers over in Cornhill, next to the Castle Tavern. Having spent so much time with Ashmole and his predicaments, he was now in a rush.

When he got back he hoped to find some time for the markedly different pamphlet he was planning for next year, plus he still had many letters to respond to, as well as answering the door to all-comers. He had better hurry if he wanted to accomplish everything; it was already after 2pm.

* * * *

Unusually for William, he was late rising on the morning of Friday 15 August 1651. The night before had been a memorable one. The Society of Astrologers of London had had their latest meeting at the Painters-Stainers Hall in Little Trinity Lane, not far from St Paul's Cathedral, and the festivities had proceeded into the early hours of the morning. They had only come to a halt after Elias Ashmole had fallen 'ill of a surfett' at 1am.

Elias, he recalled with a wince, had attempted to claim his poor health was caused by 'drinking water after venison', rather than by simple overindulgence of food and drink. It was hard to believe him: his young friend was known for his conviviality and sociability.

Ashmole had staggered home to his new wife, declaring he would have to visit Dr Wharton to free his stomach of the 'great oppression' within it. Fellow astrologer and friend Richard Saunders

THE MAN WHO SAW THE FUTURE

shouted out that he would send round a piece of bryony root for him to hold in his hand – sympathetic magic would no doubt be more efficacious for Elias than a quack's nostrums.

It was Ashmole who had organized the event after he had been chosen at the previous meeting as steward of the Society for the year. Lilly was amused to see that he had made sure to select a day when the Sun was conjunct his strongest planet Mercury: Elias did like to make a brilliant impression. He hoped the bryony root, known for its loosening properties on distended membranes and muscles, was having the desired effect. He intended to visit him later.

The meeting, William thought, had been the best yet. This year Nicholas Culpeper had spoken and had treated them to extracts of his forthcoming book, *Astrological Judgement of Diseases from the Decumbiture of the Sick* ('decumbiture', from the Latin for lying down, signified the moment the person took to their bed). Culpeper, who was in his mid-thirties, had a practice in Red Lion Street, was an expert in the medicinal properties of herbs, and was a 'master of the pestle' – a trained apothecarist.

Addressing the Society, Culpeper had stressed how the only good doctor was one who incorporated the tenets of astrological physic within his practice. 'A physician without astrology is like a pudding without fat, or a lamp without oil,' he lectured, echoing the motto of the University of Bologna's school of medicine: 'A doctor without astrology is like an eye that cannot see.'

However, in his opinion, one current problem in medicine was that the physicians' 'covetousness or laziness, or both, or something worse' would not 'suffer them to study those arts which are essential to their monopolised calling'. Most English doctors, he declared, were 'like to die dunces'. Occasionally, though, he admitted, some showed good sense. To hearty laughter, he described to his audience how a rolling pin had been used to treat a man 'possessed with wind in his belly'. The attending medic had simply rolled until the gent's fundament had sounded 'an alarm' to certify that 'ease was a coming'.

Culpeper then took his colleagues through a horoscopic example of how decumbiture worked and highlighted how doctors ignorant of astrology frequently floundered and failed their patients. One 'Doctor Dunce', he related, had told his patient she had the plague, had sworn she would die and had plied her with strong purges for a week.

But when Culpeper had cast her decumbiture (for 11 December 1647 at 11.59pm), he had diagnosed smallpox and judged she should live. The physician's incompetence, he told his fellow astrologians, could be seen in his planetary significator in the chart: in this case, it was Mars and it was conjunct the cursed Dragon's Tail.

In addition to Culpeper's lively speech, what was particularly encouraging at last night's feast was the sight of so many fresh faces. One of the newcomers, 21-year-old John Rowley from Luton, was the son of a friend of Lilly's and had written to him a month ago, telling him that he wished to attend and requesting that William let him know when the gathering would take place.

The young man had recently published his first almanac and was working on his first book (on elections and directions). He had asked for advice regarding his manuscript, and had divulged reverently that he was dedicating it to Lilly.

Rowley was not the only novice astrologer at the meeting, or the only one working on first books or pamphlets. The publication of *Christian Astrology* had had the galvanizing effect that Lilly had sought: with the language of astrology now accessible to the masses, an incredible influx into the profession was taking place. At the same time, a revival was happening: established star-gazers had been inspired by William and were keen to emulate his success.

In addition to Rowley, Henry Harflete, Humphrey Daniel, Nicholas Culpeper, William White, Thomas Herbert and Jeremy

Shakerley had all published almanacs for the first time this year. Even more were working on maiden editions for the following year, including William Ramesay, John Smith, William Crooke, George Horton, William Knight, Samuel Thurston, William Burton, Thomas Dunster and Robert Sliter.

Many of those writing books had, like John Rowley, turned to Lilly for help – requesting assistance with publication, or seeking a foreword or an endorsement. So many occult manuscripts were now being printed (both original and reissued works) that in last year's almanac Lilly had for the first time given details of those he recommended.

One of the eleven he selected was Rutland-based astrologer Vincent Wing's *Harmonicon Coeleste*. This taught 'how to calculate the motions of the planets for any time past, present or to come', and included a description of the new Copernican heliocentric model of the solar system. It was, Lilly declared, 'very useful for those who profess astrology'.

'A rare piece' was how he described his good friend Nicholas Fiske's new edition of Sir Christopher Heydon's turn-of-the-century astrology text, *Influence of the Stars and the Grounds of Astrology Proved by Demonstration*. He also endorsed works of magic describing sigil-making, and a tract entitled *Government of the World by Angels*, which had been written by the Society's speaker of the previous year, Robert Gell, minister of St Alder-Mary in London.

Everywhere Lilly had turned last night, someone had wanted to speak with him. His successes – with *Christian Astrology* and his bestselling pamphlets – had established him as the leader of his profession. George Wharton had confirmed this some months earlier when, speaking for the members of the Society of Astrologers, he wrote to patron Bulstrode Whitelocke thanking him for his support, and praising Lilly as the restorer and promoter of the mantic art.

It was 'the dexterous scrutiny & pains of Mr Lilly', Wharton eulogized, that had made astrology 'public to the benefit of the nation' and vindicated it in the face of 'the scandals of the ignorant and malicious'. For this, their leader's 'deservings' were 'indeed very great'.

Within the profession, it was to Lilly that astrologers turned when they struggled with their craft. Richard Napier wrote to him when he was unable to judge his niece's horary question of whether she should marry the man her father wanted her to. And after Ashmole asked John Booker for help with a horary, and was dissatisfied with the response, he went to Lilly the next day with the same query.

Vincent Wing had requested Lilly's assistance recently because his customer – who wanted to know where her stolen linens were – would not be content without it. In his letter to William, he explained that he had not judged the figure himself 'because she hath (not undeservedly) so good a confidence of you, and your writings, for which (I must say) we are all much obliged to you. Good Sir at her request, be pleased to honour her with a line; and she protesteth to make you part of satisfaction, if ever it be in her power. Her husband is a member of this Parliament, and one (I suppose) well known to you, and is a man that highly esteems of your singular parts.'

Lilly's public and professional status as the star science's ambassador could be seen in the high volume of letters he received. A few months ago, Abraham Wheelock, distinguished professor of Arabic and head librarian at Cambridge University, had addressed him in a letter as 'his most honour'd, & learned friend Mr William Lillie, professor of the mathematics', and had lauded him as elevated by God 'to be so happy a raiser & promoter of these admired studies in the universities and the nations round about us'.

In Wheelock's opinion, Lilly's achievements in making the learning of astrology 'more facile then all that have gone before you' were such that 'all parts of the world' should give thanks and acknowledge him. Because of his writings, the distinguished professor had begun to study astrology – at the age of 57.

A Hertfordshire clergyman, well-read in other fields, had admitted that until the publication of *Christian Astrology* he did not have the 'boldness to attempt' to study 'that hidden and sublime science of yours, wherein you have showed your excellency so many ways'. Cambridge undergraduate, Robert Billingsley, put quill to paper to say he thought William had attained the 'very height' of astrology and made himself 'as lasting as ye stars'. Nathaniel Sparke, who had wanted to learn more since reading his early almanacs, wrote to say that *Christian Astrology* – 'that perfection of the art' – was exactly what he needed.

Lilly's fame was now international. His almanacs were being translated into Dutch, German, Swedish and Danish. Followers corresponded with him from across Europe and as far afield as Barbados and America.

One gentleman from Naples, who had written in spring that year, declared that William 'approachest nearest to the divine knowledge of any'. This Italian student of astrology had visited the Corner House two years ago and had been back in contact to beg Lilly's help in furthering his studies. 'You are so noble a benefactor to our present age to publish more than most can comprehend,' he praised, 'yet you keep a reserve of the sublimest science within your own breast; or at least communicate only to such friends as you think worthiest; I would fortune invite me to that happiness.'

Now, before William left the house to visit Ashmole and enquire after his wellbeing, he turned to look at the day's mail. There were two letters to open. The first was addressed 'To the Ptolomy of this nation the famous restorer of astrology Mr William Lilly at the Corner House over against Strand Bridge this present'.

The second was written simply to 'Ye Famous Mr William Lilly' – his celebrity was so great that just his name sufficed, without an address. Choosing that one, Lilly began to read.

* * * *

Lilly was furious. The latest news in late February 1652 was that a group of ministers was trying to ban astrology. As part of an overarching plan to reform the church, raising the level of clerical and state regulation of religion, these divines had petitioned Parliament to suppress astrologers like him who gave judgement on events to come. According to their leader, John Owen, such judicial astrology was diabolical and an unlawful art.

Lilly had expected a strident response to his 1651 almanac and the usual complaints from the pulpit had ensued, but this particular attack was concerning. It came from a different and novel source, because John Owen and the group he represented were Independent ministers. More worrying still, Owen had Parliament's ear: during Cromwell's campaigns in Ireland and Scotland, Owen had been his chaplain and the men were close. It was possible that the ministers' petition could result in an Act being passed to silence Lilly's quill pen.

It was also worrying that in recent months astrology had been publicly condemned as witchcraft by minister Ralph Farmer, and that Lilly had been labelled 'that grand witch of them all'. He had felt compelled to defend himself and his craft against this serious attack. Astrologers could be arrested and charged with sorcery, according to the 1563 Witchcraft Act; the memory of the campaign of professional witch-finder Matthew Hopkins in East Anglia less than five years ago was still fresh.

Trouble was brewing from within the profession too. The swelling numbers of astromancers were gaining a name for themselves as a rabble-rousing, anti-establishment movement. He was part of the problem: a few months earlier, the Dutch ambassador had lodged a formal complaint to the Council of State about Lilly's 'abuses against their nation'.

But other prominent members of the Society were not helping matters either. Despite George Wharton's promise not to act against the Commonwealth, he did just that and was rearrested in September the previous year. He still had not learnt his lesson, however; for in his current publication he had hinted at imminent disorder. John Booker was another irritant: he had inveighed against established religious groups in his recent pamphlet, proclaiming: 'The three grand Ps, Pap[acy], Prel[ates], and Pres[byters], the pest and poison of the alphabet ... must [fall] down.'

In addition, Nicholas Culpeper was living up to his name (to be a culpeper was to be a mischief maker and to get up people's noses). *A Physical Directory* (1649), his hugely controversial Englishing of the College of Physicians's Latin directory of physic, had infuriated doctors who saw their wealth and monopoly on health slipping through their fingers.

Culpeper had made his political leanings clear from the first page of his book, on which he stated: 'The liberty of our Common-wealth ... is most infringed by three sorts of men, priests, physicians, lawyers; ... The one deceives men in matters belonging to their soul, the other in matters belonging to their bodies, and the third in matters belonging to their estates.' Is it 'handsome and well-beseeming a Common-wealth,' he asked, 'to see a doctor ride in state, in plush with a foot-cloth?'

The public loved *A Physical Directory*, making it an overnight success, but those in authority did not, calling him 'an absolute atheist' and a drunkard (Nicholas was partial to a drink and a smoke). His book was 'nonsense' and 'obscene', written only 'to bring into obloqy

[sic] the famous societies of apothecaries and surgeons'. One reviewer punningly asserted that Culpeper 'hath made Cul-paper, paper fit to wipe one's breeches with.'

In late 1650, the Council of State arrested Culpeper and forced him to answer questions about his book in front of the government's Committee of Examinations. Undeterred, Nicholas brought out a second edition. In it, his choler flared out stronger than ever: books were published in Latin and French, he fulminated, so that the 'commonalty' were 'kept in ignorance that so they may the better be made slaves of'.

Lilly had recently mentioned to Ashmole his concerns about the developing situation, but had not found reassurance in that quarter. Elias did not share his opinion on the wisdom of opening up astrology to the masses and the benefits that would bring to the profession's standing. He believed that astrology 'judiciously dispens'd to the world' (that is, to the elite in society) would bring respect for the science. His worry was that, if 'unskillfully exposed', the mantic art would become 'the scorn and contempt of the vulgar'.

Ashmole had recently expressed these thoughts in his new book *Theatrum Chemicum Britannicum* (1652), a collection of alchemical poems in English. 'Trust not to all astrologers,' he warned, 'for that art is as secret as alchemy. Astrology is a profound science: The depth this art lies obscur'd in, is not to be reach't by every vulgar plumet that attempts to found it. Never was any age so pester'd with a multitude of pretenders ... of this sort at present are start up diverse illiterate professors (and women are of the number) who even make astrology the bawd and pander to all manner of iniquity, prostituting chaste Urania to be abus'd by every adulterate interest.'

Lilly did agree that sometimes knowledge should be kept shrouded in order to protect it from 'profane hands'. He had himself, in last year's *Monarchy or No Monarchy*, concealed his forecasts representing 'the future condition of the English nation for many hundred of years yet to come' within a series of enigmatic hieroglyphics. However, he felt that astrology could not be said to have flourished within England when its secrets were kept by just a few, and he remained unrepentant about his actions in opening up the profession.

The problem now was how best to address the matter at hand. Part of him wanted to fight, but, he had to admit, another part of him was tired: he would be 50 years old in a few months' time. He had asked Ashmole on the 22nd of this month about the possibility of Mrs Lilly and himself moving to live at Elias's country home, Bradfield House, in Berkshire. It could be time to repair to the country again.

But before any such move, he must do something about the proposed ban. It was time to remind Parliament of its debt to him – of how 'in these last and worst of times' astrology was more than 'a little serviceable unto this Commonwealth'.

Only five months ago, his *Anglicus* had been used to successfully rally Cromwell's men as they fought in Scotland. He had been told how a soldier stood holding his pamphlet aloft, crying out to the troops: 'Lo, hear what Lilly saith; you are in this month promised victory, fight it out, brave boys.'

He knew what to do: his soon-to-be-published pamphlet on the forthcoming solar eclipse was sure to grab the public's attention. He would add to it a timely reminder of his services.

Chapter 5

The Dark Year

♂

Mars signifies courage, quarrels, the will and competition,
anger, survival, blood, sexuality and passions.
It is associated with iron, war, sharks, soldiers and surgeons,
nettles, garlic, ginger, blacksmiths and slaughterhouses.

At half past nine in the forenoon of Monday 29 March 1652, William Lilly, John Booker, Elias Ashmole, George Wharton, Nicholas Culpeper and other members of the Society of Astrologers were clustered together, staring anxiously heavenwards and waiting. They had been hoping for a clear sky to view the imminent solar eclipse, which was due to be visible across northern Europe. However, although it was a fine, dry, spring morning, clouds were covering the sun; occasionally they parted and a ray of sunshine peeped out to brighten the day, but this was not the weather they wanted.

The astrologers were on the roof of Southampton House, the recently built residence of the fourth Earl of Southampton, whom Ashmole knew. The Earl's magnificent new city home was right at the northern edge of London's urban development, on the fields of Bloomsbury and spanning the north side of what would become Southampton Square (and later Bloomsbury Square). The site had been chosen for today because it afforded wonderful views of the city and its surroundings. The magi were determined to see everything that was to happen on this much-heralded morning.

Down below them, the metropolis was uncharacteristically still and silent. On the ten-minute walk from the Corner House, Lilly had hardly seen a soul. No one was working; markets and fairs had been cancelled; cattle and sheep were under cover; folk were cowering in their homes behind locked doors or had taken to their beds too scared to step foot outside on what had already become known as Black Monday.

The unearthly quiet was in stark contrast to the days earlier. Then pandemonium had reigned – the wealthy loading up valuables and fleeing town; those unable to leave sealing windows with pitch; maids fetching in fresh water to hoard; usurers leaving debts uncollected. Many had been panicking: some ran mad in the streets; there were reports of breakdowns, even suicide by hanging.

Over the weekend, the courtyards and alleys echoed with the cries of the mercury men and women hawking handfuls of penny pamphlets – some astrological, some merely doom-peddling – on what to expect during the coming meeting of the luminaries. Vendors assailed passers-by with dire warnings about what would happen if their 'medicines, pill and antidotes' were not consumed; bills advertising these dubious cordials and concoctions peppered doors and posts or were pinned up in chandlers' and barbers' shops, next to the latest sheet almanacs.

Ballad singers added their voices to the clamorous city chorus. On one corner, 'The Shepherd's Prognostication' was sung; from another balladeer came the doom-laden refrain of 'England's New Bell-Man', replete with apocalyptic imagery:

Awake! Awake! O England,
Sweet England now awake ...
The dreadful day of vengeance,
Is shortly now at hand,
When fearful burning fire,
Shall waste both sea and land;
And all men's hearts shall fail them,
To see such things appear,
Repent therefore O England, the day it draweth near ...
The skies shall flame with fire,
The earth shall burn so clear.
Repent therefore O England, the day it draweth near.

During Sunday services, ministers had preached about the solar eclipse. John Swan said he had chosen to do so because of 'the great noise which I have heard among the common people concerning that eclipse of the Sun, which tomorrow in the forenoon will present itself to us.'

Fulk Bellers, addressing the Lord Mayor and aldermen of London, stressed that eclipses 'are seldom prodigious'. In his sermon, entitled *Jesus Christ the mystical or gospel Sun, sometimes seemingly eclipsed, yet never going down from his people*, he argued that it was 'heathenish' to fear eclipses, since they were not counselled against in scripture and they could be followed by good times rather than bad.

Bellers also took the opportunity to pontificate from the pulpit against astrologers, as did other ministers across the city. One divine published his denunciation in the semi-official newspaper *Several Proceedings in Parliament*; he too emphasized that eclipses were predictable, natural events.

Now, at Southampton House, the company of astrologers was beginning to grow restless. There were as yet no signs of the Moon moving to obscure the Sun's light. Lilly thought the eclipse would have begun by now: using the available astronomical tables, he had calculated that darkness would fall across the land for a quarter of an hour at most and that 'the greatest darkness' would be 'about half an hour after nine in the morning'. It was heading towards ten o'clock – were the tables wrong or had he erred in some way?

Even without this unexpected delay, he had been growing increasingly concerned about the eclipse. He had never before witnessed the country so in thrall to his prophetic words; the public's extreme reaction had taken him by surprise. It was true, as divine Nathaniel Homes had admitted this year, that astrology was 'heeded more of late with us than ever was (to our shame let it be spoken) in any Christian Commonwealth since the creation.'

Lilly also recognized that he and most of his profession were, to some degree, culpable for the mass panic seizing the nation. However, they were not the only ones – there were others at fault, including the ballad writers and cordial sellers who stoked the hysteria to its crescendo.

He had first mentioned the almost total solar eclipse at the end of last year and he could see how, in his almanac for 1652, he had set the scene and tone for other pamphleteers. The celestial event was, in his estimation, 'The most famous, the most memorable and greatest eclipse of the Sun, which our age hath beheld'.

In his discussion of the eclipse horoscope, he explained this dramatic statement, writing: 'This is the greatest obscuration the Sun hath suffered this many years; it's in a sign regal [Aries], the very first of all the twelve signs, in the very degree of the exaltation of the Sun [nineteenth degree], in that house of heaven signifying and relating unto emperors, kings and magistracy [tenth house].'

Although he stressed that people should not expect to feel the eclipse's effects immediately, he warned that England, more than any other European nation, would suffer its malignant force. This was because the obscuring of the Sun occurred in Aries, and England's founding horoscope had its Ascendant in Aries. 'Fires ... great devastations, mischiefs, and all manner of harms ... verily all, or many of these misfortunes, do seem either in part or whole, to be intended for England, and those countries subject to Aries.'

More particularly, because the meeting of the luminaries occurred in the tenth house of authority figures, he predicted 'the subversion of some principalities and powers, monarchies, kingdoms, empires, and the raising up of some one man or men, or state or Commonwealth unto a greater height of sovereignty, rule or command, than either he hath at present (if this befall a particular man) or that Commonwealth or state.'

In addition, he forecast that sheep and cattle would suffer, because the eclipse was in the sign of Aries, and the ruler of Aries – Mars – was in another bestial sign, Taurus. Also, he counselled his readers to watch out for 'much damage by water, by floods, both land-floods and high tides' – because malefic Saturn was placed on the Ascendant of the eclipse horoscope in watery Cancer.

It was John Booker who had first used the phrase 'Black Monday'. He had looked to his history books, and reading of an eclipse that 'proved so great, and fearful, the air being very dark,' that it had become known as 'black Saturday', he had written:

> Bright Sol eclips'd the nine and twentieth day
> For time to come Black Monday call we may ...

Other colleagues had followed suit, including Lilly's former student Richard Saunders, and the sombre, ominous name had caught on quickly with the public.

In the months leading up to Black Monday, pamphlet after

pamphlet poured forth from the press. George Thomason's collection of publications for March 1652 showed that a quarter of them were about the eclipse and its meaning: all the established almanac authors and some new ones as well put quill to paper. The downfall of those holding power was the most common prediction – put forward by many, including Lilly, Booker, John Rowley, Vincent Wing and Nicholas Culpeper.

Some astrologers' forecasts were coloured by their idiosyncrasies – political, personal or geographical. Henry Harflete, a Cambridge University- and Gray's Inn-educated barrister, predicted that his home town of Sandwich, on the coast in Kent, would be besieged by enormous spring tides after the eclipse. He suggested to the local commissioners for the sewers that any necessary repairs were done.

Radical politics had influenced Culpeper's two eclipse pamphlets – *An Ephemeris for the Year 1652* and *Catastrophe Magnatum*. Like his peers, he foresaw the elite cut down, but he extended this to a levelling of society. This eclipse signified a coming democracy 'or to write English, that the government shall come into the hands of the people'; these effects would be 'in full force, power and vigour throughout 1653 and 1654 ...'

The astrological theory he based his forecast on was that Jupiter was the ruler of the tenth house where the eclipse took place. As he explained, 'Jupiter delights in equality, and so do I: he delights in community and goodness ... He is a just, upright-dealing creature: he will not give all to some, and none at all to the rest ...'

Culpeper also added his feelings about the Fifth Monarchy into the mix. Since the days of the early Christians, there had existed a belief in the Western world of a golden age or paradise – a biblical fifth kingdom when Christ would come again and reign on Earth. In this new millennium, there would be no evil, oppression or cruelty, and church and government would be reformed.

During the 1640s and 1650s, there was increased speculation about when the Messiah would return: for many folk the only way to understand the turbulent events of the Civil War was to see them as part of the last days of the old world. The key question then was when the Fifth Monarchy would begin. For Culpeper, and many others, it was the movements of the stars and planets that could provide the answer.

In Nicholas's opinion, the many portentous celestial events of 1652, which included two other eclipses, a meeting of the malefics Saturn and Mars in a hotspot degree of the zodiac associated with the beginning of the Civil War, and Saturn and Jupiter opposing each other in the skies, heralded the second coming. He declared: 'the Fifth Monarchy of the world is coming, and the effects of this eclipse make way for him ... before the beginning of the year 1655 ... the government will come into the hands of the people ... Jesus Christ the Prince of Peace may reign amongst us'.

The Fifth Monarchy group, one of the radical religious sects that emerged in the wake of the beheading of Charles I, when anything seemed possible, also put out a pamphlet linking the eclipse to Christ's second coming. They proclaimed that the movements in the celestial sphere signified the levelling of all magistrates, as well as royalty – this was a forecast that tallied with their demands for radical change within society, such as law reform and the removal of taxes, tithes and distinctions between the classes.

The promotional and money-making opportunities the eclipse offered roused many other individuals to release broadsheets or booklets. Newspapers reprinted the astrologers' words; some individuals simply plagiarized the astrologers' tracts.

The Year of Wonders: or, The glorious rising of the Fifth Monarchy borrowed heavily from Culpeper's *Catastrophe Magnatum* to predict that the 'government will come into the hands of the people'. Its author foresaw the streets of London running red with the blood of its enemies and 'the stabbing of the Pope of Rome by an English-man'.

The anonymous editions were the most bloodthirsty. Playing on their audience's worst fears, they promised a panoply of disastrous events: sudden death, epidemic disease, perpetual night, universal destruction, fires, floods inundating the land and 'a great madness, raging and terrifying thousands of the people'.

One unnamed author's four-page Black Monday tract announced on its front page to expect 'malice, hatred, uncharitablenesse, cruel wars and blood-shed, house-burnings, great robberies, thefts, plundering and pillaging, rapes, depopulation, violent and unexpected deaths, famine, plague &c.' More misfortunes were listed inside, including 'abortive births, acute fevers, corruption of the air, piracies, ship-wrecks, a general murrain [disease] amongst cattle, the sacking of cities …'

Lilly published a further two booklets on the eclipse. The first, *An Easie and Familiar Method whereby to Judge the effects depending on Eclipses, either of the Sun or Moon,* contained general information on eclipses, including how to determine 'the kind and quality of events' to expect. In the second, which appeared a fortnight before the eclipse, he attempted to dismiss some of the myths surrounding what would happen and to quell the nationwide panic.

Noting that he had been asked if the eclipse threatened danger to folk labouring in the fields 'or other ways occupied without doors on their domestic affairs', he offered reassurance: 'I say it threatens no man or cattle with danger in that consideration; nor will the darkness itself be of so long or great a continuance as many imagine.'

In addition, he stressed that it was those who currently held power or authority who should watch out; the effects of the eclipse would manifest 'on men who are fully men, or of middle age, viz. from thirty unto fifty'.

This booklet proved so popular that many people complained they could not get hold of copies, as they were so 'suddenly snatched up at their first coming forth'. However, as an attempt to instil calm, Lilly's effort was unsuccessful. His few heartening words were lost within the rest of the prophecy-laden 64-page pamphlet, which was ominously entitled *Annus Tenebrosus, or The Dark Year* (PLATE 4, PAGE 118).

He gave far more space to his prediction for England of 'some man or men' attaining 'a very great dominion or power' in the wake of the eclipse. This change would come about, he forecast, 'towards March, April and May 1653 ... in good earnest the soldier and people will join in one for calling a new representative in this Commonwealth: for the Moon, who signifieth the people, eclipseth the Sun.'

Now, on 29 March, at a few minutes before 10am, birds fell silent and the men at Southampton House gazed skywards and watched as the Moon inched across the face of the Sun. Their relief was short-lived. Within minutes it became clear that this solar eclipse was, visually at least, not the spectacular event they had forecast.

The sky in London hardly darkened; the fixed stars and Mars and Venus were not visible in the firmament, as they had promised. They had been mistaken in these predictions. With a mounting sense of alarm, Lilly and his colleagues turned to leave their viewing platform. They did so to face the start of a fierce backlash against them and the art they practised.

* * * *

Lilly knew he did not have long. Thinking quickly about what needed to be done, he paced backwards and forwards across his consulting rooms. He hoped luck was on his side. Would the next knock on the door be the man who could help him evade a spell

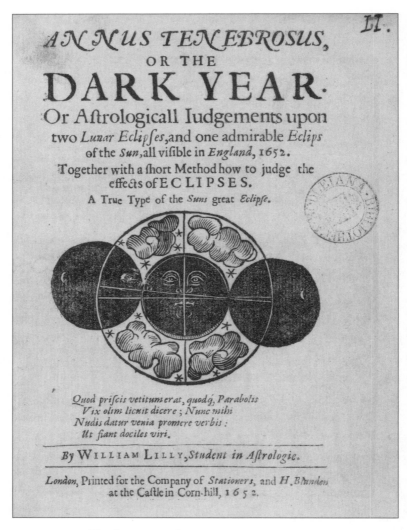

LI.

ANNUS TENEBROSUS,
OR THE
DARK YEAR·
Or Aſtrologicall Iudgements upon
two *Lunar Eclipſes*, and one admirable *Eclips*
of the *Sun*, all viſible in *England*, 1652.

Together with a ſhort Method how to judge the
effects of ECLIPSES.

A True Type of the *Suns* great *Eclipſe*.

*Quod priſcis vetitum erat, quodq̃, Parabolis
Vix olim licuit dicere ; Nunc mihi
Nudis datur venia promere verbis :
Ut fiant dociles viri.*

By WILLIAM LILLY, *Student in Aſtrologie.*

London, Printed for the Company of *Stationers*, and *H. Blunden*
at the Caſtle in Corn-hill, 1 6 5 2.

PLATE 4 The frontispiece for *Annus Tenebrosus, or The Dark Year*
(reproduced with permission of the Bodleian Libraries, the University of
Oxford, Ashm.533(2), Title Page)

in prison, or would it be a messenger with a warrant to haul him to Westminster?

The astrologer, acutely aware that his predicament was a grave one, was doing all he could to avert disaster. It was the start of November 1652 and hours earlier he had heard that one of the government's committees wanted to quiz him about the seditious nature of his latest publication. He had set out immediately to meet with the Speaker of the House of Commons, William Lenthall, who was a good friend of his, and Lenthall had wasted no time in telling him what was happening.

For the last week, members of the House had been fulminating against Lilly's most recent pamphlet – his almanac for 1653. Matters had come to a head on 5 November 1652 when the house had passed a motion, ordering:

> That the printed book, entitled, *Merlini Anglici Ephemeris*, or *Astrological Predictions for the Year 1653*, by Wm. Lilly, student in astrology, be referred to the Committee for Plundered Ministers to consider thereof: with power to send for the author, and secure him, if they see cause; and to state the matter to the Parliament, and report the same, with their opinion therein, to the Parliament.

Lenthall confirmed that the committee, which was charged with suppressing religious dissent and punishing blasphemies and heresies, was preparing to send for William and offered to help in any way he could. The two men read through the almanac together, Lenthall pointing out the passages that had most offended the Members of Parliament. It was a tricky business: some individuals had found fault with one or two sentences, others disliked every single word.

Looking through *Anglicus*, Lilly was not surprised about the anger he had stirred up. He had continued to attack Presbyterian ministers for their rants against astrology, calling them 'prick-eared' and 'half-witted' and accusing them of 'meddling in state-affairs' with their calls for a ban on astrology. However, in some places, he had also let his feelings about the present Parliament spill over on to the pages of his publication, colouring the tenor of his predictions.

His patience with the republic's ruling body had run out. His personal (unpublished) view was that the Parliament had grown 'odious'; its 213 members were 'insufferable in their pride, covetousness, self-ends, laziness, minding nothing but how to enrich themselves ... justice was neglected, vice countenanced, all care of the common good laid aside ... the army neglected'.

Lilly was not alone in thinking this. Dissatisfaction was rife across the country with the purged Parliament (which was still for the most part made up of individuals from the ruling elite who were conservative in their outlook). Record high taxes were hurting everyone; army pay was in arrears; major legal reform was in tatters; a religious solution had not been found; the army's *Agreement of the People* had been ignored and the agreed date in the *Agreement* to dissolve the purged House had slipped past.

'The greatest part of the Parliament-men,' Lilly's contemporary John Aubrey would later write, 'were cursed tyrants, and in love with their power ... they were able to grind any one they owed ill will to powder; they were hated by the army and the country they represented, and their name and memory stinks – 'twas worse than tyranny.'

The words from William that were so inflaming the government were concerned with what a forthcoming planetary opposition between Saturn and Jupiter in March 1653 presaged. The opposition took place with Saturn in its detriment in the zodiac sign of Leo, and Lilly described this placement as signifying 'a desire to rule like a company of kings or tyrants, and to back their crooked actions with force, power, impudence ... they who then sit at the stern, or do govern, will more mind filling and cramming their own purses and coffers with silver, gold and jewels, than the business or common good of the nation.' It was an astrologically astute assessment but it was also a calculatedly provocative one.

Then he went further, warning that the Saturn-Jupiter opposition in March 1653 augured that the government stood upon 'a very tottering foundation'. If Parliament tried to squeeze any more money from the nation, he forecast, 'the commonalty and soldiery would join together against them'. He declared that he was confident that:

> We of the commonalty joining with the soldier, shall assume so much liberty to ourselves, as to choose and elect such members as hereafter shall be more tender of our purses, and more liberal of their own; and we shall endeavour so strictly to call unto account each member of this Parliament, who hath fingered our treasure, that we shall leave many of them as naked as when they came out of their mothers' wombs, or when first to be members of Parliament.

After he had learnt as much as he could from Lenthall, Lilly had headed straight home. He had decided on his defence strategy during their meeting – but he had not told his friend what it was, since he did not want to make the Speaker an accessory to what he was planning. As soon as he was back at the Corner House, he put his scheme into action by sending for his printer, Mr Warren. Now, hearing a knock at his door, he hoped fervently that it was Warren.

It was indeed. Showing him in, he hurriedly apprised him of the situation and asked for his help. His tactic, he explained, was to pretend that the almanac in Parliament's possession was not actually his, but a counterfeit copy (a situation that was a regular occurrence for him, Booker and other astrologers of note). But to do this, he needed Warren to agree to produce a neutered version of his pamphlet, devoid of provocation. Could he produce six revised copies of *Anglicus* 1653 as quickly as possible?

Warren, an avowed royalist, did not hesitate. Promising to return the following morning, he left immediately to do as Lilly requested. He was true to his word and early the next day he was back pressing six new booklets into William's hand. He had, as directed, 'obliterated what was most offensive' and 'put in other more significant words'.

Thanking him, Lilly reassured Warren that he doubted the committee would call the printer to be examined. Shrugging the concern aside, Warren bade him farewell, exclaiming: 'Hang them … they are all rogues, I'll swear my self to the devil 'ere they shall have an advantage against you by my oath.'

After his printer left, Lilly considered whether he had done enough to preserve his liberty. Since meeting with Lenthall the day before, he had made sure that as many of his friends as possible would attend the hearing and speak on his behalf; and he had also planned something more specific, as we shall see. It had been a fraught 24 hours of planning, while dreading the unwanted knock on the door.

It had been a fraught year too; a dark year, even. Seven months on he was still smarting from the repercussions Black Monday had wrought; from 'the calumnies and aspersions which in so great measure, and so many weeks together' had been 'continually cast upon' him. His reputation and that of astrology had suffered badly.

Within days of the eclipse, the cantings of ballad-makers bellowing forth 'squirting ugly' Black Monday ballads were heard up and down the metropolis's streets and in the nation's market towns, while more than two dozen anonymous 'vinegar pamphlets' mocking Lilly and his peers were put into circulation. The vinegar pamphlets said it all in their titles: *Black Munday Turn'd White* (which dubbed Lilly the 'prince of prognosticators'); *The Astrologer's Bugg beare*; *Lilly's Ape Whipt* and *A Faire in Spittle Fields, where all the Knick Knack's of Astrology are Exposed to open Sale, to all that will see for their love, and buy for their money.*

A Faire in Spittle Fields had singled out Lilly, Booker and Culpeper, depicting them attempting to sell astrological tracts no one wanted. Lilly was described with his pamphlets *Annus Tenebrosus* and *Monarchy, or no Monarchy*; Booker with a 'starry globe'; and Culpeper had 'under his velvet jacket … his challenges against the Doctors of Physick, a pocket medicine, an almanack and conjuring circle'. Ridiculing the lack of darkness on the day, the vinegar tract opined:

… the sun shone glorious,
no Cummerian [Sumerian] shade
made dark our dwellings,
their predictions fail'd,
their tales prov'd fables and the people rail'd
against these jugglers whose prevarications
had filed their minds with such vain expectations.

By the weekend, further railleries were to be read in single-sheet mercuries, such as *On Bugbear Black-Monday*, and on the Sunday the pulpits thundered with the sound of ministers preaching against the celestial science and its practitioners. Minister John Gaule punned that the star-gazers' 'prodigious portending upon the last eclipse, hath proved not a little to eclipse their credit with them'.

Others enjoyed similar fun. Preaching to the Lord Mayor of London, minister Nathaniel Homes roared: 'Astrology is a lie. This last eclipse, March 29 1652 is the proof, which not proving to be so dark, gloomy and terrible, as they predicted, it hath so eclipsed their credit, that I hope you will forever take them for liars.' According to Lilly, at least 'thirty Presbyterian thumping priests, in or neer the city … belcht forth somewhat of nonsense against *Anglicus* and astrology'.

Eventually, his patience had run out. Six weeks ago, he had decided to do something about the 'singing, preaching, prating, or writing some ribaldry or other against me, the close of all ending in Black Monday'. In his address to his readers in his new almanac, instead of the usual summing up of the year ahead, he delivered a six-page defence of himself and divination.

'I hold it no dishonour to be abused in print,' he wrote, but what he was angry about was being misrepresented. He had not called the day of the eclipse Black Monday, and yet it was his name alone that was sung in the numerous satirical Black Monday ballads. 'I purposely all along in my book contradicted those who had so played the ignorant asses in print,' he declared, reminding his readers that he had reassured them the eclipse did not threaten 'danger to the labouring man or cattle in the fields'.

He refuted those who claimed that the sky did not darken at all by including first-hand accounts of the eclipse that had been sent to him from southern England, Scotland and Ireland – where the circumstances surrounding the occluding of the Sun were far more dramatic. 'I could not see to write … I assure you for almost one quarter of an hour it was extremely dark, so that we saw Venus, and many other stars, in the north hemisphere', a gentleman in Waterford communicated; another correspondent declared: 'it was the darkest morning … ever seen by any man in Scotland.'

A citizen of Dalkeith was moved to write: 'Riding this morning betwixt Edinburgh and this town, in the time of the eclipse, I saw such an appearance of doomsday as not before; the poor people throwing away all, casting themselves on their backs, and their eyes towards heaven, and praying most passionately, that Christ would let them see the Sun again, and save them.'

It remained to be seen whether or not these defensive words would help repair his professional reputation. However, it was his other comments in this current *Anglicus* – those that were causing so much offence politically – that were his priority now. Finally, as the light faded on another day and the feared knock on the door still did not come, Lilly relaxed slightly; the stars were shining favourably – his scheme was in place.

He had hatched his plot just in time. The next day a warrant to seize him was issued and he was marched to Westminster (with the amended pamphlets secured out of sight in his pocket). Interest in his case was strong: 36 committee members turned up, instead of the usual five or so. William was pleased to see there were some to speak for him.

Calling him to stand, the committee chair began proceedings by handing him a copy of *Anglicus* and asking him if he had written it. Lilly inspected the original version of his pamphlet intently, turning it this way and that, examining each of the pages. After a minute or so, raising his head, he pronounced: 'This is none of my book, some malicious Presbyterian hath wrote it, who are my mortal enemies, I disown it.'

Taken by surprise, the committee men turned to each other, muttering, unsure what to do next. Lilly reached into his pocket and with a flourish pulled out his six newly printed pamphlets. Handing them over for scrutiny, he declared: 'These I own, the others are counterfeits, published purposely to ruin me.'

Perplexed and thwarted, the committee fell silent; 'not one word was spoke a good while.' After some time, finding their voices, they began a heated debate about what to do next. Unfortunately for

William, although friends spoke on his behalf, including Hugh Peter, the majority were not convinced by his ruse and wanted to imprison him – in either Newgate or the Gatehouse gaol.

As they argued about where to lock him up, a Mr Brown of Sussex, known as 'the Presbyterian beadle', spoke up. He reminded his fellow committee men of the correct procedures to follow, pointing out that, at this time, Parliament did not send prisoners to either of these penitentiaries, but rather the sergeant-at-arms took them into his custody. If they wanted to make Lilly a prisoner, they would need the services of the sergeant-at-arms. Hearing this, William smiled inwardly: the Company of Stationers, who controlled the production of almanacs, had bribed Brown to speak for him (his price was a copy of John Foxe's popular 16th-century *Book of Martyrs*).

Before the committee could decide their next move, MP and Council of State member Walter Strickland stood up. He had been waiting to lend his voice for a while. Now, seeing how determined the committee was to place Lilly under restraint, he chose his moment to declare:

> I came purposely into the committee this day to see the man who is so famous in those parts where I have so long continued [Strickland had been ambassador to Holland for many years]; I assure you his name is famous all over Europe: I come to do him justice. A book is produced by us, and said to be his; he denies it; we have not proved it, yet will commit him. Truly this is great injustice. It's likely he will write next year, and acquaint the whole world with our injustice; and so well he may. It's my opinion, first to prove the book to be his, 'ere he be committed.

After a pause, Strickland continued more forcefully:

> You do not know the many services this man hath done
> for the Parliament these many years, or how many times,
> in our greatest distresses, we applying unto him, he hath
> refreshed our languishing expectations; he never failed us
> of comfort in our most unhappy distresses.
>
> I assure you his writings have kept up the spirits both of
> the soldiery, the honest people of this nation, and many of
> us Parliament-men; and now at last, for a slip of his pen (if
> it were his) to be thus violent against him; I must tell you,
> I fear the consequence urged out of the book will prove
> effectually true. It's my counsel, to admonish him hereafter
> to be more wary, and for the present to dismiss him.

Strickland's supportive words were to no avail. Ordered to
stand, Lilly was committed to the custody of the sergeant-at-arms
and marched away. But before he was taken from the room, a message
arrived, halting the proceedings – the commander-in-chief of the
army, Oliver Cromwell, had requested to see Lilly, whom he had never
met. When Cromwell arrived, he looked at William 'for a good space'
but did not comment before turning and leaving.

Then, just as Lilly expected to be led away, a young clerk of the
committee spoke out. 'Where's the warrant? Is it signed?' Realizing that
it was not, he asked: 'Will you have an action of false imprisonment
against you?' At this, the committee had to give up – William was
released and returned to the Corner House until the committee
could procure the necessary signature. That night, according to Lilly,
Cromwell approached one of his friends and admonished: 'What
never a man to take Lilly's cause in hand but yourself? None to take
his part but you? He shall not long be there.'

The following day, with the correct documentation in place, William was taken and lodged in the sergeant's custody. Every day, for nearly two weeks, he tried to secure his release by delivering a petition to the committee, but the committee men, who were mainly Presbyterians, refused his petition each time.

On the thirteenth day of such attempts being made, Joseph Ash was appointed chairman, and he agreed to listen to Lilly's plea – though he warned him to get messages out to as many of his friends as possible to attend the hearing. Later in the day, the committee met again to hear the petition. Plenty of William's circle attended, including the extrovert and outspoken politician Sir Arthur Hesilrige, and Major Richard Salway. For two hours they argued his cause; finally, worn down by his supporters, the committee bailed him.

A weary but unrepentant William walked back to the Strand. His liberty was his own once more, and he intended to appreciate it. The first thing he was going to do was leave London for a period. Although he had turned down Ashmole's generous offer of living at Bradfield House, he had realized in the last few months that he would like a country home of his own to retire to.

He had always liked the property he had lived in during the 1630s, when he had fled London for a short time, and he had recently bought it and its accompanying land. It was a large house (of thirteen hearths), surrounded by eighteen acres of parkland, in Hersham, a village in the parish of Walton-upon-Thames, Surrey – not far outside the city. Tomorrow he was going to install himself there to get the rest he needed.

However, his imprisonment had proved useful. One of Bulstrode Whitelocke's friends, John Rushworth, had visited him during his time in custody. Rushworth, who was an intelligence man for the Council of State and a former secretary to the council of the army, as well as to General Fairfax and Cromwell, had told him that 'the army would do as much as Lilly had predicted unto the Parliament'.

Remembering this, William could not help smiling as he returned to the Corner House. If Rushworth was correct, Lilly's so-offensive forecast that Parliament stood upon 'a very tottering foundation' and that 'the soldier' was about 'to call unto account each member of this Parliament' was shortly to come true.

* * * *

William sat back, stretched and looked around. He was in his study in the Corner House – home to his vast library of occult manuscripts, which he had been collecting for over 20 years. He had spent days on end in his youth searching through bundles of tracts in the streets of Little Britain and on the stalls in St Paul's churchyard, always with an eye for the choicest stellar offerings. Even before his passion for the star science was ignited, he had loved books, and in this office these two joys of his came together: he had passed plenty of happy hours here in communion with his world.

There were more than 200 books to feast your eyes on. All the great authors were there: medieval classics including Guido Bonatti's *Liber introductorius ad iudicia stellarum* ('A Book of Introduction to the Judgement of the Stars'); the Arabic master Albumazar's *De Magnis Conjunctionibus* ('The Great Conjunctions'); and later works including the collections of nativities from Luca Gaurico (*Tractatus astrologicus*) and Girolamo Cardano (*De Judiciis Geniturarum*), as well as Andrea Argoli's recent medical treatise, *De Diebus Criticis et de aegrotorum decubitu* ('Critical Days and the Decumbiture of the Sick').

His study also housed his array of sidereal instruments: a celestial globe; an armillary sphere (one of the oldest observational instruments, used to tell the time or ascertain when constellations rose); and an astrolabe – a two-dimensional mapping of the three-dimensional starry firmament – which was used to tell the time, measure the heights of stars and buildings, predict sunrises and sunsets, survey land and cast horoscopes.

These exquisite and intricate items were both the tools of his trade and symbols of his status. Armillary spheres (*armillae* is Latin for 'rings') were metallic models of the universe: at the centre was a ball, representing the Earth, which was encircled with rings denoting the circles of the celestial sphere; the thickest was the ecliptic. The skeletal spheres of the heavens were a symbol of worldly dominion, as well as of Astronomia and Urania, the personifications of astronomy and astrology.

The astrolabe (the name means 'star-holder') was said to be the most important mathematical instrument ever invented, and to own one was a mark of learning, affluence or position in society. Lilly's was engraved with London's latitude (51°). His astrolabe also incorporated an equatorium and astrological volvelle on the reverse side. The equatorium was used to calculate past or future planetary positions. The volvelle was a series of concentric moveable discs which when rotated was used to calculate the positions of the planets, and compute the ruling astrological sign at a particular time.

From downstairs, William could hear the sound of Ruth, the new Mrs Lilly, moving around, breaking into song every now and then. It was the last weekend in October 1655, and they had just celebrated one year of marriage. This time he was in love with his wife; he had 'married her for love not for money'. His second spouse had died in February 1654; at which, he admitted, he had 'shed no tears'. Eight months later, on 26 October, he wed 26-year-old Ruth.

Ruth was a good match for him, despite being nearly three decades younger – not least because, with her birthday just days apart from his, their earthy Taurean Suns were happily conjoined. She possessed a sound intellect, was sociable and a generous hostess and had an obliging disposition and deportment; Lilly described her as being 'so totally in her conditions, to my great comfort'.

In William's opinion, his natal Jupiter in Libra signified Ruth. This said a lot about his feelings for her: Jupiter was the strongest planet in his horoscope, the Lord of the chart and the ruler of his Pisces Ascendant; Ruth represented the best of him. He had never been happier in his home life.

The same could not be said of Ashmole whose marriage was again proving problematic. At the start of July 1654, after only three years of wedded life, Elias and his wife had separated. It was Mrs Ashmole who left: she went to live with a friend (initially) and began court proceedings against her husband.

What she was claiming was intolerable behaviour on her husband's part, on the grounds of his adultery or ill temper – which could entitle her to receive alimony from him. Alarmed at this prospect, Ashmole was doing all he could to effect a reconciliation and requested repeatedly that she move back in with him. Lilly had also spoken with her, but as yet to no avail.

Earlier in the year, Ashmole had been arrested and imprisoned for twelve days; he had not revealed why. He had committed adultery with a number of women and, since the Adultery Act of May 1650, this was typically punishable by a spell in prison (although the death penalty was legally possible). In June, the situation between the warring spouses had become so bad that William offered Elias the Corner House to lodge in; he had accepted gratefully and resided there when he needed to.

Lilly had opened his home to another friend in need over the last couple of years. The man in question – John Gadbury – was here now on this October day in the study. Gadbury was 27, and apprenticed to a tailor in Strand Bridge – minutes from the Corner House. 'Pale and swarthy', he had piercing hazel eyes, lots of dark brown curly hair, 'a full broad visage' and a 'strong well-knit body of a middle stature', which tended towards corpulence.

He had made Lilly's acquaintance in the months after Black Monday: at this time Gadbury had recently published his first astrology pamphlet – 'a vindication of Mr Culpeper, Mr Lilly and the rest of the students in that noble art' – and was working in spare moments with his uncle Timothy on updating *Hartgill's tables* (a book of astronomical tables, originally published in 1594, detailing the nature and position of the fixed stars).

On hearing about the Gadburys' plan to produce recalculated star tables, which would be very useful for all astrologers (as the position of the stars in relation to the equinox changed incrementally owing to precession), Lilly had immediately offered the use of his study and books to support and speed the work.

As the two men got to know each other, William warmed to the trainee tailor: Gadbury, although not university-educated, was a bright young man and passionate about astrology, just the kind of gentleman Lilly had hoped to welcome into the profession; and so he took him under his wing.

Over the last two years, Gadbury had enjoyed Lilly's patronage: he was introduced to his circle of colleagues and friends; was taught astrology by him; and worked as his tailor, making him new clothes and mending his old. Mrs Lilly also benefited: in the months after the Lillys' marriage, Gadbury made Ruth a petticoat trimmed with silver lace; while William requested a coat, a cloth suit and a fustion-lined doublet.

The Gadburys' amended tables were due to be published shortly, complete with a glowing foreword from Lilly, as well as commendations from Booker and Wharton. Encouraged by the support and endorsements he had received for his first project, Gadbury had recently told Lilly of his plans for his next book,

Genethlialogia, or the Doctrine of Nativities, which would focus on natal horoscopes. William agreed to provide another foreword and opened up his library once more. It was good to have young blood in the profession; it was possible Gadbury could be the man to take up his mantle of leadership in due course.

The manuscript Lilly was working on now, on this late autumn day, was his almanac for next year. This *Anglicus* for 1656 was not as outspoken as usual (and that of the previous year had not been either). In both he acknowledged holding back from publishing all that astrology revealed to him because he felt it was unsafe for him to speak his intentions fully.

'*Anglicus* could tell more, but he loves not a prison,' he had stated in *Merlinus Anglici Ephemeris* 1655. Today, composing next year's edition, he had written about how he wanted 'to retire and end those few years we have yet remaining in quietness, peace and tranquillity' – he did not want to 'run our self upon the rocks'.

He recognized that part of the reason for his new-found reticence was the change in his personal circumstances; he simply did not want to upset his happy home. But his lack of candour was also related to the recent regime change. In April 1653, as Lilly had predicted, the make-up of Parliament changed dramatically.

During the interregnum, Oliver Cromwell had been mediating between the army and Parliament whenever there was a disagreement between the two bodies – such as John Owen's scheme to reform the church and outlaw astrology, or the plan in late 1649 to establish Presbyterianism as the national religion. By spring 1653, tension about whether the purged Parliament would dissolve itself, as it had promised, had reached a peak and Cromwell had to persuade the army's officers not to expel the Members. He repeatedly told the MPs to hurry up, but on 20 April he lost patience and called in soldiers to clear the House and forcibly dissolve Parliament.

Then, in December 1653, after an interim 'little Parliament' had not proved successful, a new Council of State elected Cromwell Lord Protector of the Commonwealth. In the months after its inception, the first Protectorate Parliament pushed through several ordinances including ones enabling some reform of both the law and the structure of the national church (astrology's legal status was not altered). However, at the start of the current year (1655), after MPs had begun to discuss the creation of an alternative militia under their sole control, an angry Cromwell again dissolved Parliament.

Since spring of the present year, the newly installed second Protectorate Parliament had behaved in a far more authoritarian manner. Individuals who had been involved in a royalist rebellion in March were either executed or transported to the West Indies, some of them without trial; leading army men were commissioned as major-generals with unprecedented wide powers and duties including suppressing insurrections; and Cromwell's Secretary of State John Thurloe now controlled an enlarged spy network, as well as wielding the power to censor the press.

One consequence of this new approach was the disappearance of many newsbooks; the ones that survived were government journals written in a bland, timorous style. In addition, with rumours everywhere of plots to assassinate Cromwell, anyone speaking out against the Protectorate could expect to be treated roughly. Royalist astrologer John Heydon, who had fought for the King during the Civil War, was imprisoned when he foolhardily prophesied that Cromwell's death by hanging was imminent.

George Wharton's continued railing against the Protectorate earned him another stint in jail in 1655. He had gathered a welter of evidence, in the form of celestial omens and astrological portents, to reveal how change was coming. A swarm of bees ('those monarchical creatures'); a shower of blood in Poole in the southwest of England;

and Christ appearing in the sky, albeit overseas, had led him to conclude that the 'time is at hand ... for every one to have his right'. He had been imprisoned in Windsor Castle since mid-June and had not yet managed to secure his release, although he had been allowed out on parole in August.

With this in mind, William had not repeated a cryptic prediction that he had made in 1645 about the length of Cromwell's reign. Then, in his *Collection of Prophecies*, he had forecast that the one who followed the White King (Charles I) – 'the Chicken of the Eagle' (a reference to Cromwell's former status as a smallholder of chickens and sheep) – would not enjoy a long reign or old age.

Using 'the clavis [key] of the more secret astrology', Lilly had prophesied: 'The Chicken of the Eagle ... shall obtain the kingdom of Britain, but not with the sword, but by mediation, treaties, love of the British,' and 'shall be the only man of his race allotted to sway the British sceptre ... But to their perpetual sorrow, he reigns but a few years; for our wise man tells, he shall not live till he is old ... In his best of years he unwillingly leaves the world, nation and crown, to the extreme sorrow of the people.'

Since Cromwell had become Lord Protector, Lilly had referred to this earlier prediction by using similar phrasing to describe him. The Lord Protector, he wrote in his introduction to his 1655 almanac, was 'the first of his race, who hath enjoyed so great a power'. Later, referring to Cromwell as his Highness, he added: 'Consider our position, how unsafe it is, how dangerous it would be for us to speak our intentions fully ... he [Cromwell] hath many enemies, our self as many; but both our lives are in the hands of God ...'

William had also been shaken by a recent war of words that had ended with the death of his sparring partner – the minister Thomas Gataker. Their argument in print had begun in earnest in the months after Black Monday, when the 79-year-old Gataker had published a 192-page booklet *Against the Scurrilous Aspersions of that grand Imposter, Mr William Lillie.* Gataker had been incensed by Lilly's 'raving and ranting rhetorick' against Presbyterian ministers, as well as by the very nature of astrology itself.

A flurry of paper bullets followed between the two in the ensuing year, with the furious minister accusing Lilly of 'lewd and lowd lies' and 'shameless slanders', and of having a 'malicious and murtherous mind, inciting to a general massacre of God's ministers'. But when William forecast that Gataker would die in August 1654, noting in his observations for that month *'Hoc in tumbo jacet Presbiter et Nebulo'* ('Here in this tomb lies a Presbyter and a knave'), and Gataker had died at the very end of July 1654, he felt chastened; there were professional ethics that he always strove to uphold and in this instance he felt he had not done so.

Commenting on this episode, in a postscript in *Merlinus Anglici Ephemeris* 1655 (written four months after Gataker's death), he promised: 'We will henceforth meditate heaven, and are resolved never hereafter to meddle in point of controversy, or to take notice in print, either of the person or failings of any particular man'.

Other events in the summer of 1654 had also served to put Lilly more on his guard. In July, a young woman, Anne East, who was a returning customer, visited him. Could he help her again? Her husband Alexander's ten waistcoats (valued at five pounds) had been stolen. She had consulted with other astrologers, but had not been satisfied with their responses. Could he judge if her family would get its property back?

Lilly did as she wished. Casting the horary chart for the event, he judged 'that the goods would not be recovered', and charged her his usual fee – half a crown. Giving judgement on stolen goods was, of course, strictly illegal, but it was part of his usual professional practice and, at the time, he thought nothing of it.

At the start of this year, 1655, however, he heard that Mrs East had pressed charges against him. He was accused of being 'in contempt of the laws of England' and was indicted to appear at Hick's Hall sessions house for the justices of the peace in St John's Street, Clerkenwell, to respond to the suit. Over the next few months he waited: the bill against him was presented to the jury at three separate sessions and was thrown out each time, but on the fourth attempt it was accepted and he was summonsed to appear.

By this time, he had come to suspect that the lawsuit was a set-up – concocted by two aggrieved Presbyterian ministers determined to silence him. His suspicions were confirmed when he appeared at Hick's Hall: many of the justices of the peace present were Presbyterians and they were 'much for her'. However, Lilly had ensured he had support too: he 'had procured Justice Hooker to be there, who was the oracle of all the justices of peace in Middlesex'.

The sessions began with the prosecution producing two female witnesses – former clients of Lilly's. The aim was to show how he regularly contravened the 'Against Conjuration, Witchcraft and Dealings with Evil and Wicked Spirits' Act of 1604 by using occult practices to recover what was lost or stolen. Unwittingly, though, the result was a demonstration of his skill and accuracy as an astrologer.

Under oath, the first woman told the court that after her son ran away and she was 'in much affliction of mind for her loss', she visited Lilly to find out where he was. His judgement was that 'he was gone for the Barbados', and she would hear of him within thirteen days; which, she said, she did.

The second witness, on being sworn in, described how she had consulted with Lilly regarding her husband, who had been missing for two years. The astrologer correctly identified that he was in Ireland and informed her he would return home at such and such a time. Her spouse had 'come home accordingly', the woman told the hearing. Once more, Lilly had been accurate in his judgement.

When he was asked to stand and answer questions, Lilly admitted 'the taking of half-a-crown' for his judgement of the theft. But then, given the opportunity to speak further, he produced his cherished astrology guidebook. Holding *Christian Astrology* up high, he stated to the court: 'Some years before I emitted this book for the benefit of this and other nations; it is allowed by authority, and has found good acceptance in both universities; the study of astrology is lawful, and not contradicted by any scripture.' After a pause, he concluded by swearing: 'I neither had, or ever did, use any charms, sorceries, or enchantments related in the Bill of Indictment.'

When it was Mrs East's turn to speak, the unexpected happened. At first, she was very coherent in her accusations, and gave a 'very ingenious speech', which Lilly felt the ministers behind the case had written for her and she had memorized word for word. But when his counsel, Recorder Green, moved to question her, her statement began to fall apart and she began to sound more and more muddled.

She complained that after she had visited Lilly, 'she could not rest a nights, but was troubled with bears, lions, and tigers'. Pressed to describe the colours of these beasts that had so terrified her, she then denied seeing any. Counsel destroyed her as a credible witness, declaring her 'an idle person, only fit for Bedlam [the notorious mental hospital]'. Answering all other objections, Green concluded: 'Astrology is a lawful art.' The jury dismissed the case.

Thinking about all this now, as he prepared to finish his 1656 *Anglicus*, Lilly knew he had been fortunate once more: yes, justice had triumphed in the Mrs East case, but it was another warning to him about the dangerous ground he stood on. He had annoyed many over the decades, and although stalwart friends surrounded him, he was minded to be cautious for a time.

In addition, he had not forgotten the words he had written in 1644 in *England's Prophetical Merlin*. 'In the years 1659 and 1660,' he had predicted, 'our nobles and gentlemen root again ... here's almost a new world, new laws, some new lords: now my country of England shall shed no more tears ...' Considering this and his new-found domestic harmony, he was content to put forward a more temperate *Anglicus* for 1656.

* * * *

For once, Lilly was unsure how to proceed. It was autumn 1659 and he was preparing his almanac for the next year. He had already outlined his major prediction for 1660: the stars foretold that very great and high designs were in agitation; 'a general revolution is at hand', he had written, adding that February would witness the first 'news of clandestine plots to disturb England's authority ... one grandee is near attaining a high preferment ... he may carry it, the vulgar people are for him; so are many serious persons'.

Adding more detail on the timing of this great change, he had forecast: 'Near this month of March, April, May or June, ariseth some person to much honour in the esteem of the commonalty, and a strong desire there will be in many persons of quality to be popular ... we shall find that in the months of March there will be some signs or significations of what may be expected, but rather in clandestine consults, than otherwise, for no perfect discovery seems distinctly to manifest itself until May towards the latter end'.

He was satisfied with this prediction, but it was what he needed to write next that was causing him to procrastinate. He had to write an apology, admitting he had made an astrological error. At the start of September 1658, Oliver Cromwell had died unexpectedly – though this was not Lilly's problem. He had foreseen Cromwell's death and had alluded to the Lord Protector's short reign and demise as much as he could, while taking care not to earn another prison sentence.

In his almanac for 1658, he had wished Cromwell 'long life and eternal happiness in the next', but added that he could not say anything more about the government because it would provide 'nothing pleasing unto the times, or of safety unto the author'. Pointing out that Mars, Cromwell's signifier in England's ingress chart for the year, was conjunct the malefic *Cauda Draconis* and London's Ascendant, he cautiously noted sad news for the country at the time that Cromwell died.

But what he had not forecast was that in April of this year, Cromwell's successor – his son Richard – would unexpectedly resign, abruptly ending the Protectorate years of government. Instead, in last year's almanac, Lilly had continued to predict wonderful things throughout 1659 for Richard as Lord Protector; he had got it wrong and he had to try to repair the damage.

Eventually he decided what to say, stating simply: 'It's as much the part of an ingenious person to acknowledge an error, as it is to write a truth: we solemnly profess our mistake concerning Richard late Protector.' He hoped this would suffice.

That done, there was another serious matter to address: putting aside his manuscript for the moment, he moved to pick up his copy of John Gadbury's *Doctrine of Nativities*, which had been published the previous year. Opening the book, he turned to the flattering foreword he had written for Gadbury (and to which he had signed his name).

'I must acknowledge it [*Doctrine of Nativities*] the most accomplished work of this subject I ever yet beheld in any language or author,' he had enthused, adding that he was 'heartily glad to behold so learned a production from an English man; the essential verity whereof, shall manifest unto posterity for many ages, the high worth and indefatigable industry of the author.'

Reading his words again, he was incensed. He could still hardly believe what had happened: since the start of the year, Gadbury had produced pamphlet after pamphlet mocking Lilly, questioning his abilities, attacking his work and all he stood for, calling him a poisonous snake and accusing him of endeavouring to bring about his ruin and doing him 'many superlatively-manifest injuries'.

Now, shaking with rage, William took up his quill and scrawled across the page 'an impudent rogue' and, several times, 'monster of ingratitude' (recalling the words William Shakespeare had King Lear call his daughter Cordelia). Then, unable to contain himself, he obliterated his signature, stroke by stroke, from beneath his glowing recommendation. Finally, he picked up his almanac manuscript: he knew now how he wanted to answer Gadbury's betrayal.

Chapter 6

Hieroglyphics of Hell

2|

Jupiter signifies higher learning, wisdom, philosophy and religion,
luck, the principle of expansion, travel, largesse and joviality.
It is associated with tin, the liver, judges, ministers and scholars,
universities, publishing, dolphins, the oak and nutmeg.

Inside Westminster's Gatehouse prison, where he had been since first light, William Lilly stood tall as he was ordered to take the Oaths of Allegiance and Supremacy to the Crown. Now, all he had to do to put this 'stinking place' behind him was pay the extortionate costs of 37 shillings and he would be at liberty again. 'But for how long', he wondered, as he finally walked free.

It was January 1662, and England was no longer a republic. After moves had been taken towards the Restoration in February 1660, Charles II had returned triumphantly to assume his place as the nation's monarch on 29 May 1660.

From the start, the new King's reign was characterized by its attempts to promote conformity and consensus in order to prevent further rebellion and upheaval. But to create such a land of 'right-thinking' individuals – who supported Charles and monarchy – radicals, supporters of the old regime and other dissenters had to be suppressed and the press restricted.

The regicides – the men directly involved in Charles I's beheading – had been hanged, drawn and quartered. Cromwell's body was desecrated: disinterred from its tomb in Westminster Abbey, the rotting corpse was taken to the Old Bailey, where the death sentence was passed on it, before it was hanged in a shroud at Tyburn. The final act was to chop off Cromwell's head and impale his skull on a pole above Westminster Hall.

Regarding the vexed issue of religion, the new government immediately began the process of reinstating episcopacy (which had collapsed on the eve of Civil War), and Charles had initially preached toleration for non-conformist sects. But after an uprising by a group of Fifth Monarchy men at the start of 1661, leaders of all the radical sects were targeted, their leaders and members arrested and their meetings disrupted. Now, during 1662, the Act of Uniformity, which would reject the toleration of dissent, was being drafted.

For many, including Lilly, the first few weeks after the Restoration were a tense, anxious time, as the newly installed government rounded up those with links to the republic and questioned them about their activities. The astrologer was taken into custody within weeks of the new King entering London – the new Parliament wanted to examine him about the identity of Charles I's masked executioner.

Before he could give evidence, though, the committee, which included Presbyterians, took the opportunity to punish him for his past, asking 'several scurrilous questions' and affronting him grievously. Fortunately, Richard Pennington, the son of his old royalist friend William Pennington (whom he had always supported successfully), was present, and he persuaded many to support Lilly.

When allowed to speak, William divulged all he knew. Two Sundays after the beheading, Cromwell's then secretary Robert

Spavin had invited him to dine with Spavin and other compatriots: 'their principal discourse all dinner time,' he told the committee, 'was only, who it was that beheaded the King; one said it was the common hangman; another, Hugh Peter [Lilly's friend, who would be executed later that year for his role in Charles's death]; others also were nominated, but none concluded.'

Then, after dinner, Spavin took Lilly aside and said: 'These are all mistaken, they have not named the man that did the fact; it was Lieutenant-Colonel [George] Joyce; I was in the room when he fitted himself for the work, stood behind him when he did it; when done, went in again with him; There's no man knows this but my master, viz. Cromwell, Commissary Ireton and my self.'

For holding this knowledge, Lilly was placed under arrest for two days, and was then discharged – paying £6 and 40 shillings. But his tribulations were far from over. Over the next few months, a series of offensive, anonymous pamphlets was published. One detailed how he had answered the charges of knowing the King's killer and got off because of whom he knew. Another read as if it were a confession from him: Lilly, this pamphlet claimed, had said 'my constant club-fisted friend John Booker hath promised to hang himself' and had pledged to swing with Booker to keep him company.

The title of a third pamphlet said it all – *A declaration of the several Treasons, Blasphemies and Misdemeanours acted, spoken and published against God, the late King, his present Majesty; the Nobility, Clergy, City, Commonalty &c. By that Grand wizard and Impostor William Lilly ... Other wise called Merlinus Anglicus: presented to the right honourable the members of the House of Parliament: in order to secure him from acting any further villainies against His Majesty.*

This unnamed author accused Lilly of being Parliament's puppeteer prophet: he was 'the States Balaam, who for hire would curse and bless for the rump [the purged Parliament] and Oliver according to their respective instructions and dictates, upon pretence of art, wherein he hath no more skill than the beast his predecessor rid on [the biblical diviner Balaam rode on a donkey].'

The pamphlet went on to allege that William had played a role in inciting Charles I's slaughter, had slandered him, had been involved in arranging his executioner, had abused the clergy and nobility, and had praised Cromwell. Concluding on an ominous note, it blamed him for all the ills of the nation and demanded appropriate punishment:

> For that he is looked upon as the only man now in England guilty of all our sufferings: it is therefore referred humbly to the consideration of this right Honourable Parliament, whether it be not very just that he should be excepted as to his estate, which is considerable, being the wages of his arch-villainies, and he himself kept in such security as the good people of England may be secured from his infernal actings.

Lilly did what he could to soothe the situation. In his 1661 almanac, he swore humble 'obedience and loyalty unto his sacred Majesty' and promised not to ever 'hereafter in our writings give the least occasion for any to carp at us'. Warming to his theme, he added: 'We have in the prognostick part of this year's predictions omitted all smart [acerbic] language, and all bitter epithets, whether against men or nations, which might occasionally have given offence or occasioned a just complaint unto his Majesty or counsel, for so by his several declarations we are commanded.'

Now, as he made his way back to the Corner House, it was clear from the events of the last 24 hours that these efforts had met with limited success. This latest arrest, which had taken place in the early hours of the morning before he had yet stirred from bed, was part of a campaign to seize known 'fanatics' – the avowed foes of the new conservative regime. He had been rounded up with about 60 other supposed fanatics (some ex-soldiers, others ordinary civilians), and had been marched in darkness to Whitehall by a sergeant and 34 musketeers.

After a hellish few hours housed in one large room, surrounded by swearing, smoking, sleeping and snoring men, Lilly received the writ for his imprisonment and, with a 'miserable crew of people', was taken to the Gatehouse by a 'whole company of soldiers'. Arriving there, Lilly spent three hours in the open air, before being transferred upstairs; his fellow prisoners on one side were 'a company of rude, swearing persons, on the other side many Quakers', who had 'lovingly entertained' him. He secured his release by involving his old friend Sir Edward Walker, the clerk to the Privy Council, who argued successfully for him on the grounds that there was no particular information against Lilly, and therefore no good cause to hold him.

The problem he was presently facing was twofold. Firstly, there was his personal reputation as a troublemaker and rabble-rouser: he was a known parliamentarian sympathizer, was given to making anti-authoritarian comments in print, and had demonstrated considerable power in influencing and inciting the public.

But the situation went beyond the personal: it was also a matter of the profession's changing status. The circumstances of his arrest this morning highlighted this. He and his profession were now seen as a counter-culture movement and labelled fanatics – grouped together with the nation's radical sects. Worryingly, both the ruling elite and the general public held this damaging view.

This perception of the profession had existed since the early days of the interregnum. In the aftermath of Black Monday, an anonymous pamphleteer had published *Lilies Banquet: or, the Star-Gazers Feast* (1653), which imagined that the Society of Astrologers welcomed 'all Sects and sorts of persons, both Presbyterians, Independents, Anabaptists, Quakers, Shakers, Seekers and Tearers'.

Although overstated by many, there were actual connections between the astrologers and the radical sects. There were long-standing business relationships. Lilly's and Booker's clients included various Levellers, including Richard Overton, and a number of Anabaptists. John Lilburne's wife regularly consulted Booker, as did Ranter William Rainsborough (brother of the more famous Thomas).

Outside Lilly's and Booker's consulting rooms, the associations continued. Some astrologers espoused radical religious views. John Gadbury dallied with radicalism in the early days of his astrological career, embracing the Ranter sect and its leader Abiezer Coppe, who was infamous for preaching naked and fornicating with multiple women (both at the same time and serially). Nicholas Culpeper had expressed his Fifth Monarchist views openly; astrologer Nicholas Gretton led a non-conformist sectarian group, while Thomas Webb was a Ranter who had been tried for adultery.

The radicals themselves expressed considerable interest in astrology. Fifth Monarchist John Spittlehouse described it as the princess of the sciences and Lilly as 'the prince of astrologers'. Digger leader Gerrard Winstanley and preacher John Webster advocated the study of the star science. Both Laurence Clarkson, the Ranter and ex-Leveller, and John Pordage, leader of the Behmenists sect (followers of the German mystic Jacob Boehme), took up astrology. One 1652 pamphlet simply noted how astrology was 'a study much in the esteem of illiterate Ranters'.

Now, in the Restored kingdom, where everything connected with religious and political radicals was being rejected, astrology and its practitioners might well be pushed beyond the pale too. Lilly's arrest today, as a 'fanatic' and for unspecified reasons, was symptomatic of a general tendency; it was extremely concerning. Head bowed,

William hurried home.

The problem was how best to counteract this view of the mantic art; was it possible? Lilly would be 60 years old in less than four months' time; he had been talking about retiring for the last five years. But the question was, who would replace him at the helm of the profession?

* * * *

It was summer in the city, June 1664, and Lilly was sitting in Child's coffee-house, in Warwick Street, next to St Paul's churchyard and the cathedral. Child's was one of London's newly fashionable coffee-houses, where he often met to sip coffee served in a copper or tin dish (and costing a penny), enjoy conversation with the men around him (women were not permitted, unless employees) or sample the latest reading material displayed on the communal tables – newsbooks and newssheets, almanacs, gazettes and handwritten manuscripts.

At this moment, he was alone in the sociable noisy room, reading a letter from fellow astrologer Thomas Heydon. The contents of the missive reassured him, but they saddened him too. Heydon had contacted him to proclaim his support and friendship for him and to apologize: he was 'heartily sorry' that he had listened to John Gadbury's malicious insinuations about Lilly and had let his judgement be clouded.

Heydon had written that he had, initially, 'believed the serpent', rather than William. But he had changed his mind. 'I have found him false in a trifle over £10 I lent him, the fellow is foolish,' he divulged. Now he agreed with Lilly: Gadbury was 'the scorpion that studies mischief'.

The scorpion was a reference to Gadbury's natal horoscope: his Ascendant was in the zodiac sign of Scorpio, the scorpion, which was associated with duplicity and intense passions. But Heydon was also alluding to the way in which Lilly had retaliated to Gadbury's vitriolic personal attacks at the end of the interregnum.

In his 1660 almanac, William had commented repeatedly and pointedly on Scorpio's more negative aspects, calling it 'the deceitful sign', 'the malevolent sign', the 'treacherous violent sign'; but he had chosen not to rise to any of Gadbury's other accusations, noting with restraint that 'we should make ourselves ridiculous to answer a boy'.

It was still unclear exactly what he had done (at some point between 1658 and 1659) to offend the younger man. Gadbury's complaint at the time was that for seven years he had been 'as a servant' to him, venturing 'both his pen, purse, and person, for, and on his behalf'. But, Lilly's 'great and mountain promises and pretences' had 'vanished on a sudden'.

To William's knowledge, the potential act that could have triggered Gadbury's temper was his lukewarm review of his former student's *Doctrine of Nativities*. In his 1658 *Anglicus* he had included his usual round-up of new publications, and while he had described others variously as 'this excellent and elaborate work', 'admirable and wonderful' and 'excellent and useful', he had simply described Gadbury's book as 'useful'. He had also neglected to name the proud, young man as the author.

Gadbury's printed attacks on Lilly had continued apace at the start of the Restoration and made the latter's life more dangerous by reminding the public what he had forecast about Charles I. Regarding these comments, William had maintained a dignified silence.

But in late 1662, Gadbury had published a book, *Collectio Geniturarum*, in which he accused his former patron and tutor of plagiarism. Lilly, he asserted libellously, had used the unpublished work of a man named Edward Gresham to produce his bestselling 1644 pamphlet, *England's Prophetical Merlin*.

Hearing of this, Lilly responded. He felt it was necessary: not only was Gadbury libelling him in the book, he was also spreading slanderous rumours among the astrology profession, doing what he could to convince colleagues, such as Heydon, that their leader did not deserve to keep his place at the pinnacle of star science.

Lilly turned to Ashmole for legal advice; and his old friend, who was still on cordial terms with Gadbury, resolved the matter. Ashmole found proof that Edward Gresham could not have written what Gadbury claimed he had because Gresham had died before the time under discussion. To deprive Gadbury of any grounds for undermining this defence, Ashmole also engaged a notary to issue a legal certificate confirming the facts. Confronted with this evidence at the start of the year, Gadbury was forced to desist from libelling and slandering Lilly further.

Professionally, Lilly's reputation was recovering: Heydon's letter today pointed to that. He had also made sure to broadcast in his current almanac the information Ashmole had uncovered, adding: 'we are not disposed to quarrel with our quondam [former] tailor, the most ingrateful person living'.

Despite all the quarrels, he was still the profession's acknowledged leader, the magus the others deferred to in points of theory or turned to when they had a problem. In October 1662, when John Booker's younger son Samuel (then apprenticed) went missing for a few days, an anxious Booker immediately turned to Lilly for help.

Writing to William, he confided that both his sons were causing him concern: 'was any man so vexed with his children males,' he asked, 'as I have late been?' He had recently sent the elder son John to Barbados, and now, he said, he was 'perplexed with another'; his wife was 'afraid some misfortune or imprisonment is come to him'. Could his old friend reassure him, did the stars show Samuel in danger? Lilly replied straightway and was able to say his son was safe.

However, although he remained the authority figure within the Society of Astrologers, it was a profession in flux. The Society had not met for over three years – the last occasion being a meeting at the Corner House on 24 October 1660, when a young clerk to the navy and justice of the peace, Samuel Pepys, had been allowed to attend.

Pepys later wrote in his diary:

> So to Mr. Lilly's with Mr. Spong, where well received, there being a club to-night among his friends. Among the rest, Esquire Ashmole, who I found was a very ingenious gentleman. With him we two sang afterwards in Mr. Lilly's study. That done, we all parted; and I home by coach, taking Mr. Booker with me, who did tell me a great many fooleries, which may be done by nativities, and blaming Mr. Lilly for writing to please his friends and to keep in with the times (as he did formerly to his own dishonour), and not according to the rules of art, by which he could not well err, as he had done.

It had been a convivial evening, but since then the annual meetings had not occurred, in part because of changes in members' circumstances. Lilly was not resident in London as much as in previous years – his inclinations tended more now to the quiet life in Hersham with Ruth (he had been made church warden in his parish of Walton-upon-Thames). Nicholas Culpeper had died unexpectedly in 1654. Royalists Ashmole and Wharton were thriving under Charles II's reign and had far less time to devote to the Society. Wharton, who during the years of the republic had been reduced to working for Ashmole, collecting his rents, had been appointed Royal Paymaster after 1660 and no longer actively practised astrology.

Ashmole had made himself known at court within days of

Charles II returning to London, and was soon presented to the King. Knowing of his monarch's interest in alchemy and scientific discoveries, he gave him copies of his three alchemical books (*Fasciculus Chemiculus, Theatrum Chemicum Britannicum* and *The Way to Bliss*), as well as two items from his collection of curiosities (one was a foetus preserved in liquid in a jar; the second a dried specimen of conjoined twins 'preserved with spices').

Ashmole's approaches had the desired effect. He now held office as Windsor Herald, with royal leave to assemble and transcribe any documents he wanted (and had had his portrait painted in the robes of this office). In addition, he gained the important position of Comptroller of the Excise – charged with overseeing one of Charles's main sources of income. Ashmole was a man of means, power and patronage. Mindful of his good fortune, he had employed Booker and fellow astrologers Thomas Streete and Richard Edlin as clerks in the Excise Office.

Ashmole was also involved with a new society, which gathered in London at the end of 1660 with the aim of founding 'a college for the promoting of physico-mathematical experimental learning'. The group had since taken the name the Royal Society, meeting at Gresham College (the site of the Society of Astrologers' original gathering more than a decade earlier).

In Ashmole's opinion, the creation of the Royal Society was presaged in a conjunction of Jupiter, planet of higher learning, and Saturn, planet of tradition and authority, in the 'fiery trigon' of Sagittarius; the new philosophers, he thought, would 'illustrate, enlarge and refine arts like the tried gold'.

The Royal Society gentlemen could often be found in the local coffee-houses – Child's, where Lilly was now, or Garraway's, which the latter and his friends also frequented. Both groups of men found themselves well served by Child's and Garraway's. Child's was convenient for sampling the pamphlets and books for sale in St Paul's churchyard. Garraway's was not far away, just a short walk eastwards on the corner of Exchange Alley (a busy thoroughfare of shops built in 1662) and next to the Royal Exchange (a two-storey shopping emporium where one could purchase astrolabes, globes and other sidereal and mathematical instruments).

It was not unusual for the regular, if not daily, trip to the coffee-house to result in members of the two clubs meeting. Through Ashmole, Lilly became acquainted with a number of the Royal Society men, including the curator of experiments, Robert Hooke; the astronomer and mathematician, Jonas Moore; and the antiquary, John Aubrey. The astrologers and the would-be scientists had much in common: they all had a deep curiosity and desire to further their understanding of the world, and they shared a common academic heritage – astrology, astronomy and mathematics were originally the same art.

Within the walls of the coffee-house, the two professions enjoyed the cut and thrust of intelligent repartee and debating matters of current interest. Topics included: the latest research on astral weather prediction; recent blood transfusion experiments; Hooke's work with microscopes; natural phenomena such as earth tremors; whether outbreaks of fire and plague were linked to the movements of the planets; cures by sympathetic magic; prognostic dreams; the effect of the Moon on brain structure; how to determine longitude at sea; spontaneous generation; the life cycle of fauns and dryads; the physical explanation of prodigious births; how to prove the existence of witches, spirits and incorporeal substances; as well as the latest personal and political news.

Lilly enjoyed these friendships and the stimulating conversations. Ashmole's new club was thriving and he was happy for him. But there were worrying disparities between Lilly's own profession and the Royal Society fellows.

Astrology's reputation continued to be one of discord and dissent – its practitioners were still known for loud, public quarrels and an anti-establishment stance. In contrast, the new science appeared to offer a safe haven, philosophically speaking – one that was very attractive for a nation desperate to put the division and bloodshed of war behind it.

The Royal Society owed its appeal to a variety of factors. One was the scientists' social and educational background. The all-male members came predominantly from the genteel classes (making them socially respectable), and they were university-educated, and hence viewed as part of the intelligentsia.

A second factor concerned the public face of the Society – how its members were understood to comport themselves. The closed nature of their experiments and the specific, neutral language in which they reported their findings in journals meant that, in the main, they presented a polite, well-mannered and non-confrontational face to the public. Most disagreements were hidden from public view.

Thirdly, the aims of Ashmole's new organization were aligned with those of the Restoration regime. The Society, which had taken care to ensure the patronage of Charles II, concentrated in its experiments on reaching a shared view of the empirical facts. Such agreement, the Society sensibly argued, would be a stabilizing force for society; and its insistence on consensus helped to secure the scientists' reputation for stability.

As for the astrologers, events in the previous few years had not helped their cause. The year before (1663), astrologer John Heydon was imprisoned for publishing treasonous literature – he had written a book suggesting that Charles II was a tyrant. During the same period, Lilly was falsely accused of supplying a forecast to help a group of anti-government plotters led by the Fifth Monarchist man Colonel Henry Danvers. The new regime had also investigated him, in the early days of the Restoration, for helping parliamentarian General John Lambert in his plans to escape from the Tower of London.

The increased social complexity of his profession was also proving problematic. Lilly's aims for *Christian Astrology* had been accomplished: he had opened up the profession to all individuals, irrespective of their background. He had made astrologers of millers (William Hills), grocers (William White), ropemakers (Robert Sliter), bakers (Richard Saunders) and tailors (John Gadbury and Henry Coley), as well as physicians (Robert Wittie), parsons (Robert Sterrell) and Cambridge scholars (Robert Billingsley and Richard Hunt), to name just a few of his protégés.

There were even female astrologers. In 1658, Sarah Jinner became the first female astrologer to publish an almanac. In her 20-page pamphlet, with its frontispiece depicting her in elegant dress, fine jewellery and coiffed hair, she defended her right to be heard. 'You may wonder,' she wrote,

> to see one of our sex in print especially in the celestial sciences: I might urge much in my defence, yes, more than the volume of this book can contain …
>
> But, why not women write, I pray: have they not souls as well as men, though some witty coxcombs strive to put us out of our conceit of ourselves, as if we were but imperfect pieces, and that nature intending a man, when the seminal conception proves weak, there issues a woman … nay, let me tell you, we have had a pope of our sex, named Pope Joan, which the best historians do not deny …

As proof of feminine ability she listed Queen Elizabeth I, the Amazons, and 'rare' female poets, including Margaret Cavendish, Duchess of Newcastle; and she added, 'it is the policy of men, to keep us from education and schooling, wherein we might give testimony of our parts by improvement'. Jinner's hope, she wrote, was for a time when 'the people may have some eminent champion to assert their liberties'; government, she reminded her readers, 'hath no other foundation than the humour of the people'.

Her almanacs followed the traditional format, albeit with a feminine tone. In her month-by-month analysis of the ingress chart for 1658, she forecast that 'Venus being in Scorpio, I fear me that the naughty wantons of our sex, as well as the other sex, will be peppered with the pox, and if so, woe be to your noses; it is malignant to catch it at this time.'

Dashes of womanly lore distinguished her work. There were 'the good housewives observations' – handy hints about what should be done in the fields and kitchen each month. And there was information on female wellbeing, such as a recipe for 'a syrup to stay the immoderate flux of the terms [menstrual period]'. 'Things by nature cool, which move the terms are the seeds of small endive, of melons, of gourds, of pompeons [pumpkins], cucumbers and lettuce, of which pessaries may be made, to use in the womb, but,' she stressed, 'have a care you put a string to them, to get them out again when you please.'

Keen that 'our sex may be furnished with knowledge', she also provided guidance on reproduction. If 'a confection to cause fruitfulness in man or woman' was needed, she recommended using the warming herbs 'cinnamon, mace, cloves, galingale, long pepper'. Other remedies included a treatment for witchcraft-induced impotence, a powder made from a 'red bull's pizzle' to quell female ardour, and rue for men to make them 'no better than a eunuch'.

With women in its ranks and all social classes accounted for, astrology had become a democratic profession. But the key question was whether this was beneficial in the current political climate. Other astrologers were expressing Elias Ashmole's long-held worry that opening up access to the star science would make it 'the bawd'. John Heydon had recently bemoaned how 'The late years of the tyranny admitted stocking-weavers, shoemakers, millers, masons, carpenters, bricklayers, gunsmiths, porters, butlers, etc. to write and teach astrology and physic.'

Lilly's plan to improve the profession's intellectual vitality and its respectability was not working. Plus, he was still searching for a suitable candidate to be at the helm. Gadbury continued to push for the position, but he would never be able to secure his senior's support.

However, there was one young man who had recently come to Lilly's attention – Henry Coley – and here he was entering Child's on this summer's day. Seeing William, Coley smiled and headed over to join him. The two men liked each other, and here was a chance to cement their friendship.

* * * *

The first hieroglyphic depicted a huddle of lawyers, gowns on their backs, hats on heads, and fear and consternation etched on their faces. They were surrounded on all sides by threatening hordes of soldiers and civilians with military and rustic weapons – pitchforks, swords, guns and cudgels. This was 'the law near tottering'.

On the next page, four crowns lay scattered on the ground, 'some sideling [turned on their side], some turned upside down, some rising'. Beneath, two ministers were in free fall – one tumbling headfirst from a split-asunder, jagged-edged pulpit, the second with arms splayed out seeking balance as his broken box of a pulpit swayed vertiginously on the edge of collapse. The image revealed 'the ministry, sinking, failing, declining, but not extinguished', and the nobility for the most part losing 'that power they once had', until some family rose again to have 'more esteem and countenance than now they have'.

The third page of the hieroglyphics depicted 'a person of honour' standing beneath a blazing sun encircled by four pens fixed in clouds. He was dressed 'in a gown as a man versed in counsel' and he held a sword aloft 'as a commander in arms'. A crown was placed upon his sword, rather than on his head – 'intimating that though he wear not a diadem on his head, he hath it in power and command by the sword'. The word *Pax* – 'peace' – was written under his weapon. This was Oliver Cromwell, the Lord Protector, who, though he 'hath been a soldier, is now a gown-man, or a man of counsel.'

According to Lilly, the nineteen enigmatic designs in *Monarchy or no Monarchy*, which he had published fifteen years earlier in 1651, were representations of 'the future condition of the English nation for many hundreds of years yet to come'. When they were first seen, they had puzzled many, and still did. Among them were biblical images of plenty and famine, and much else besides – plump and wizened oxen; strange creatures fighting lions; moles scurrying after crowns; moles tied to dragons and attacking them; angels trumpeting below the Sun and Moon; ships sailing up a wide river; and men with swords whispering and plotting.

In recent weeks and months, two of the portentous 'enigmatical types' had become notorious. They were the reason why William was now, in autumn 1666, back at Westminster, again being interrogated by the government. The first of these pictures was sinister and doom-laden: in the top half 'people in their winding-sheets' lay on the ground; the image beneath showed men wielding pickaxes and shovels to dig multiple graves. This hieroglyphic, Lilly would later admit, represented 'a great sickness and mortality'.

The second was even more striking (PLATE 5, PAGE 160). A pair of naked people faced one another, clasped in each other's arms, upside-

PLATE 5 William Lilly's hieroglyphic predicting the Great Fire of London, 1666 (reproduced with permission of the Bodleian Libraries, the University of Oxford, Ashm.553(1), Illustration 11)

down. One female, one male, their features and physique matched exactly, suggesting twins. Dangling from the sky, they hung without support as a large, roaring fire blazed directly beneath them, the flames lapping at their hair.

Five men attended the conflagration. All seemed to be trying to extinguish it – pouring water from flasks, jars and buckets. Some wore hats and had swords, another was shown with a turban and a quiver of arrows. Above the two figures on the left, the skeleton of a blank horoscope (the only direct astrological reference to appear in any of the nineteen drawings) hinted at the underlying meaning of this cryptic picture.

These images had become infamous because they painfully described how plague and a monstrous fire in the metropolis had afflicted the nation in the last sixteen months. Bubonic plague had struck first. Carried by the fleas of infected rats, this highly infectious and deadly disease first appeared in England in late 1664 in the coastal town of Yarmouth (after moving westwards across Europe during that year).

By spring 1665, London's citizens started to fall ill, and in June, as a heat wave had engulfed the city, the sickness spread like wildfire: by August nearly 3,000 people a week were dying; by the end of the year in London there were around 100,000 fatalities.

As the 'horrible and devouring plague' raged, William at first stayed in London to do what he could to help the sick and dying. He was visited by 'very many people of the poorer sort,' who, although ill, 'were so civil, as when they brought waters, viz. urines, from infected people, they would stand purposely at a distance; I ordered those infected, and not like to die, cordials, and caused them to sweat, whereby many recovered.' At the start of July, though, William and Ruth left the stricken capital for the relative safety of their Hersham home.

Lilly had predicted 'pestilence or plague' in his 1665 *Anglicus*, writing: 'Here is approaching great fatality unto mankind by sudden surfeits, evil airs, the little pox and great French pox.' He singled out the summer months as the time when London should be 'afraid of the sickness, or some such pestilential disease … the heavens seem to weep and mourn for the great slaughter of mankind now or near these times.'

He had also foreseen the plague and fire nearly 20 years earlier – in his almanac for 1648. Then he had warned how 'sundry fires and a consuming plague' would afflict London and those 'inhabiting in her' in the year 1665 'or near that year'.

He had not been the only astrologer to make this prophecy. In a 1664 pamphlet, Richard Edlin had outlined his theory that the great conjunction of the two superior planets Jupiter and Saturn in October 1663 augured a great plague in 1665 and fire in 1666. Edlin had observed, as others had done before him, that plague had come in the wake of Jupiter-Saturn conjunctions in 1603 and 1623; hence he predicted that 1665 too would be a plague year.

The Great Fire began on Sunday 2 September 1666, as a long, hot summer straggled to an end. Starting in a baker's shop in Pudding Lane in the east of the city, the flames were fanned further by a strong easterly wind, and swept quickly through the crowded, narrow streets, crammed with overhanging wooden buildings.

London burned for four days, reducing five-sixths of the city to smoking rubble and claiming countless lives: the booksellers and publishers who lived and worked around the print mecca of St Paul's churchyard saw their shops demolished by the conflagration and their livelihoods ruined. Lilly's house at the east end of the Strand narrowly escaped: the blaze roared down Ludgate Hill heading for the Fleet river and towards the West End, but by evening on Wednesday 5 September the wind had changed and the fire had damped down, saving the Strand.

Ashmole's chambers in the Middle Temple also came under threat. On the second day of the blaze, as the fire had moved closer to his residence, a worried Elias arranged for his collection of rarities (books, old manuscripts, ancient coins, medals and pictures, including a 1647 oil painting of Lilly which the latter had given him) to be taken by boat to his friend, Mrs Tradescant, who lived on the opposite side of the Thames in south Lambeth. Fortunately for him, the fire stopped at Temple on 7 September.

In the aftermath of the disaster, speculation was rife in London about what or who had caused the inferno, and the belief grew that it had been started deliberately to destabilize the city and monarchy. Suspicion fell first on foreigners – namely, the Dutch and French with whom England was at war – and then on the Catholic community amidst talk of a papist plot.

As conspiracy rumours escalated, unrest increased and the government began to fear rioting. In an attempt to quell disquiet, Charles II announced in public that the fire was due to the hand of God and asked his Privy Council to investigate all conspiracy allegations.

It was then that Lilly's name was mentioned. It was widely believed that the hieroglyphic depicting the twins dangling over the fire was a prediction of London's recent woes, for it was common knowledge that the zodiac sign associated with London was Gemini – the twins. Was there any 'treachery or design' behind this image?

However, it was not just his hieroglyphic prophecies that had brought Lilly to the government's attention: an incident that had taken place earlier in the year had also triggered its interest. At the start of May, a group of men – former parliamentarian soldiers, led by a Colonel John Rathbone – was found guilty of conspiring to kill Charles II. As part of the intrigue, the men had planned to set fire to the city, and the day they had settled on to do this was Monday 3 September when there would be a full moon.

After the fire, in mid-September, Samuel Pepys remarked in his diary that 'it was very strange' that this plot scheduled for 3 September had so closely coincided with when the blaze had actually started. The committee investigating the fire thought so too and was determined to find out more. Lilly was implicated since, according to *The London Gazette* for 29 April 1666, Rathbone and his men had chosen the date of 3 September because the astrologer's almanac declared this was 'a lucky day' for such a plot, as the planet then ruling 'prognosticated the downfall of monarchy'.

A summons to appear before the 'Committee appointed to enquire after the causes of the late fires' was issued to William on 22 October. It ordered: 'That Mr Lilly do attend this committee on … the 25th of October, 1666 at two of the clock in the afternoon in the Speaker's chamber, to answer such questions as shall be then and there asked him'. It had been signed by Member of Parliament Robert Brooke, chairman of the committee.

By chance, Lilly was in London when the summons arrived. He had moved permanently to Hersham in July the previous year, after he had left the plague-ridden capital. He often returned, though, to meet with his friends, and it was on one of these visits that the summons was delivered.

Prior to his attendance, he consulted his best friend. He was worried about what could happen. Could Elias help? Ashmole reassured him he would do all he could. After this meeting, the younger man spoke with as many of the committee members as possible to persuade them to Lilly's cause. Now, on the day itself, he was there by William's side as his fellow astrologer was taken into the Speaker's chamber.

Ordered to stand, Lilly faced the special parliamentary

committee. Robert Brooke began the proceedings by reminding the government men about William's booklet of hieroglyphics. 'Mr Lilly,' he stated, 'this committee thought fit to summon you to appear before them this day, to know, if you can say any thing as to the cause of the late fire, or whether there might be any design therein, you are called the rather hither; because in a book of yours long since printed, you hinted some such thing by one of your hieroglyphics.'

William replied carefully. He could not say anything about the cause of the fire, but he could relate what had led to the drawing of the inferno hieroglyphic. 'After the beheading of the late King,' he explained, 'considering that in the three subsequent years the Parliament acted nothing which concerned the settlement of the nation in peace; and seeing the generality of people dissatisfied, the citizens of London discontented, the soldiery prone to mutiny, I was desirous, according to the best knowledge God had given me, to make enquiry by the art I studied, what might from that time happen unto the Parliament and nation in general.'

Because of the nature of his revelations, to which he had come 'by the more secret key of astrology, or prophetical astrology', he 'thought it most convenient to signify my intentions and conceptions thereof, in forms, shapes, types, hieroglyphicks etc, without any commentary, that so my judgement might be concealed from the vulgar, and made manifest only unto the wise.' In doing this, he insisted, he was 'imitating the examples of many wise philosophers'.

Hearing this, the committee pressed for more information about the drawings. Lilly replied: 'Having found, sir, that the city of London should be sadly afflicted with a great plague, and not long after with an exorbitant fire, I framed these two hieroglyphicks as represented in the book, which in effect have proved very true.'

When another committee member asked him if he foresaw the precise year, he paused, and then lied. 'I did not,' he said, 'nor was desirous, of that I made no scrutiny.' Before he could continue, another committee man spoke up: could Lilly say anything, he asked, regarding the rumours about a design behind the fire, and if so, who was to blame?

'Sir,' William replied, 'whether there was any design of burning the city or any employed to that purpose, I must deal ingeniously with you, that since the fire, I have taken much pains in the search thereof, but cannot or could not give my self any the least satisfaction therein, I conclude, that it was only the Finger of God; but what instruments he used thereunto, I am ignorant.'

The matter of whether or not Lilly was connected to Colonel Rathbone's plot to slay Charles II was not introduced. This was because the *London Gazette* had got its facts wrong: Lilly had not referred to 3 September as a propitious time to bring down the monarchy.

Rather, it was public knowledge that 3 September was seen as a fateful day because it was the anniversary of Oliver Cromwell's victory over the Scots at both Dunbar in 1650 and at the Battle of Worcester in 1651, as well as the date of his death in 1658. It was likely that the day had been chosen for these reasons.

Overall, Lilly was lucky. Thanks to his considered responses and Ashmole's work behind the scenes, he was treated with great civility by the committee. Having heard him answer all the questions put to him, the committee appeared satisfied with what he had said, and dismissed him. Two days later, a 26-year-old French national, Robert Hubert, was executed by hanging at Tyburn, London, for starting the fire. He was innocent.

* * * *

Lilly was sitting in Nando's coffee-house in Temple Bar surrounded by lawyers, students and legal clerks. It was late October 1667 and he had come up to London for pleasure and business. Seeing Elias

Ashmole was to be the social part of his trip – he had lots to discuss with him, and they were due to meet shortly in Nando's.

At Ashmole's request, he had recently started writing his autobiography. The two men had been shocked earlier in the year when John Booker had died. Write your life story down now, Elias urged him, and William had begun. He was planning on updating his friend today regarding his progress.

He also had two astrological analyses to present to Elias. The first was the chart William had drawn up for the moment King Charles II had placed the first stone in the rebuilding of the Royal Exchange, which had been destroyed by the Great Fire. The second Elias would be keen to discuss – the subject was his own nativity.

So far, Lilly had completed about half of the detailed analysis of Ashmole's birth chart and today he had brought the annual 'revolutions' of the geniture for 1667 through to 1680. Elias had plenty to look forward to. He could expect to enjoy 'much estimation in his office', which would lead to his obtaining 'much respect at court and elsewhere'; plus there was the promise of 'much good will and friendship from women or Venerian persons be they male or female'.

The latter would be of particular interest to Ashmole who, although living again with his wife after her bid to obtain alimony had failed, continued to have an eye for other women. However, there was a warning: Lilly urged that he should be careful 'to suspect some discord from a woman, or no great success if he travel northwards'.

As well as meeting Elias, William was in the city to complete the process of getting his latest almanac printed. He had just picked up his 1668 edition from the licensers and was about to read it thoroughly to see what changes had been made – something he wanted to do before speaking with his old friend.

Unfortunately for him, the press restrictions that the Restoration government had introduced with the aim of suppressing political and civil unrest had resulted in the path to publication becoming far more difficult. The Licensing Act of 1662 meant that all books were now required to be licensed. This meant that officially sanctioned newsbooks were the only ones available (the *London Gazette* became the only licensed newspaper) and pamphlets like his were heavily edited. Charles II and his courtiers, like many of their predecessors, were concerned not to see their personal and political vulnerabilities exposed in public, nor to have the nation read rabble-rousing prophecies.

At the start of the Restoration, the position of licenser of almanacs had immediately become a royalist one. John Booker was initially replaced by George Wharton, but shortly afterwards the new regime appointed Roger L'Estrange as state licenser, with a warrant to 'seize all seditious books and libels, and to apprehend the authors'. L'Estrange soon became notorious for the severity of his censorship – smashing presses and jailing printers, authors, booksellers and publishers associated with dissenting material.

Lilly did not escape L'Estrange's wrath. His manscripts now routinely returned to him 'all corrupted by the illiterate marks' of the man he called 'old Crackfarts'. In his opinion, the licenser 'macerated, obliterated, sliced and quartered' his copy.

His response so far to this was to make it clear to his readership when he had been silenced. He left blank spaces and ellipses revealing where his intended words had been purged, or he inserted comments to the effect that he could not say more 'lest we might give offence'.

Apart from this, there was little he was able to do and he, like all the other almanac compilers who wanted to remain in print, was forced to produce suitably watered-down publications. For himself, this had meant declaring Charles II to be merciful; others stressed their allegiance to the crown and love of monarchy; while Vincent

Wing wrote that a solar eclipse in 1661 augured 'tranquillity, peace and happiness' for both the government and the clergy. John Ward, the vicar of Stratford-upon-Avon, noted in his diary that the majority of England's astrologers did foresee the Great Fire, but the Restoration government's restrictive censorship policy had prevented these dangerous prophecies from being aired.

Now, as Lilly looked through his 1668 almanac, his irritation grew. Old Crackfarts had censored him heavily again. L'Estrange had expunged references to the shock and scandal of the previous year when the Dutch navy had caught the government off-guard – the Dutch had sailed up the Medway river, captured the fort there, burned much of the English fleet at anchor and towed the flagship back to Holland as a trophy.

The mention of 'venerian passions' being at the 'root of all the mischief lately happened' had been cut out – because it would be understood as a comment on Charles II's reputation as a womanizer, with numerous mistresses. A prophecy that a king would die in February had also been deleted.

His monthly forecast for April of 'Novel grumblings or reprisings, like to cause a commotion' in Ireland and of adversaries appearing against 'kings and rulers' had been removed; all that remained was his comment about what would happen after the Irish altercations, when the nation, he had foreseen, would be 'in a thriving and peaceable condition'.

Comments about the possibility of fire in the metropolis in September and November had been erased, deemed far too worrying in the light of the Great Fire two years earlier. The September observations should have included: 'we fear in London some small contentions and hope the magistrates will be careful for prevention of fires, or such like thereof the beginning of this month.' All that L'Estrange had allowed was: 'many comfortable aspects towards the end of this month, giving great content to all sorts of people, by news of the returned or returning in many rich ships'.

William was livid as he put down his manuscript. Old Crackfarts was ruining his work and destroying his livelihood. These neutered publications, shorn of their feisty and controversial comments and prophecy, were not as popular with his readers. His annual almanac sales had fallen during the Restoration years – from their peak of approaching 30,000 in 1652 to around 8,000 in 1664.

He was not the only one who was suffering. Many astrologers had given up producing pamphlets in the current political climate: the total numbers of almanacs had dropped from a peak of nearly 100 authors in the 1650s to half that by the late 1660s. The Restoration government's drive to maintain power via ideological domination – deciding what was talked about and what was not – was working. He and his fellow professionals were being wounded in the process.

But what could he do? There must be something. Then, hearing his name as he sat there in the coffee-house, William looked up. It was Ashmole calling to him, with a great smile on his face, and looking like a man in the prime of his life.

That is it, thought Lilly: I will urge Elias to use his influence to persuade the authorities to replace L'Estrange. Perhaps that might work. At least he had to try it, or his print empire would disappear. Standing up, he reached out to greet his old friend.

Chapter 7

The Last Magus

ħ

Saturn signifies authority, discipline, time, tradition and control,
the material, boundaries and the principle of contraction.
It is associated with old men, lead, hemlock and the yew tree,
bones and teeth, stone masons, graveyards and death.

Lilly's frown of concentration deepened. Sitting in his study at home in Hersham, he scrutinized the pages in front of him. Reaching the end of the pamphlet, he sighed, took a deep breath and prepared to read it again: he wanted to be sure he had understood the full import of what John Gadbury was suggesting in his just-published almanac for 1671.

If he was correct, Gadbury – who was now 42, the age he had been when he had made his print debut and established himself at the vanguard of his profession – was not only outlining his grand vision for astrology in the coming years, but was demonstrating that he was the man to steer astrologers forwards in this new direction. It was the first serious challenge to William's leadership.

Gadbury's plan was an ambitious, collaborative research project to develop and refine the celestial science. 'That astrology may be more accurately understood, for the improvement of our knowledge in the latter,' he had written, 'I will presume humbly to propose … that astrology may be divided into sundry particular parts, and distributed to several persons well skilled therein, to advance and improve …'

In Gadbury's opinion, the six areas of research the investigative star-gazers should focus on were the weather, medical astrology, elections, world astrology (in particular, fires, plague and wars), market fluctuations (foreign and domestic) and nativities; there was no mention of horary.

The aim for each experimenter was to gather as much relevant raw data as possible – for example, the genitures of individuals 'eminent in any faculty, whether of law, physick, heraldry, philosophy, music, the mathematicks' – and then 'draw up their observations into axioms or aphorisms, putting them into distinct classes, as the several subjects shall require; and communicate them for public good.'

Noting that he would be happy to do any of the work involved, Gadbury concluded his proposal by promising that 'This method observed, and encouraged, would be a means to bring astrology to that degree of perfection, that scarcely any art at present can boast of; and possibly teach us a surer way to the discovery of the truths of nature, then hath been hitherto practised by the greatest philosophers in the world.'

Lilly had known for some time that his rival's philosophy of astrology inclined towards the experimental method. Gadbury's aim of creating a 'body of astrology' had begun with the publication in 1662 of his compendium of birth data, *Collectio Geniturarum*. Then, three years later, he asked readers of his almanac to send him the birth data of boys born between 1657 and 1659 (together with the notable events of their lives), and the birth data of males born on either 4 or 5 September 1664. Gadbury's audience responded enthusiastically, and the would-be leader of the astrological profession now had approaching 10,000 nativities; this was his 'army'.

Gadbury was not the first to believe that progress for astrology lay in gathering a comprehensive body of sidereal information from which to discern patterns and rules. The collators of figures of heaven across the centuries had had similar ideas, including Girolamo Cardano, who in 1534 was the first to show the public the value of amassing such a collection. More recently, in 1630, Abbott Orazio Morandi had been building a bank of politically explosive astrological intelligence until Pope Urban VIII had stopped him.

The tailor-turned-astrologer was also far from alone among his peers in holding this particular belief about how to refine and perfect the star science: it was the fashionable way of thinking. Royal Society man John Aubrey, a mutual friend of Gadbury and Elias Ashmole, had recently begun assembling nativities, and was focusing on those 'famous in learning, wealth, valour etc'. These included his many friends within the elite literary and scientific circles he moved in – such as playwright John Dryden and Royal Society members Robert Hooke, Christopher Wren and Jonas Moore.

Aubrey hoped that his method of obtaining information 'from their own mouths' would 'get a supellex [apparatus] of true genitures … which the astrologers may rely on' (it would instead form the basis of his gloriously gossipy and celebrated collection of biographies, *Brief Lives*). He proclaimed astrology to be 'worth any gentleman's serious observation' and expressed the belief that 'we are governed by the planets, as the wheels & weights move the index of the clock'.

Two of Gadbury's colleagues, John Goad and Joshua Childrey, had been observing and recording correlations between planetary movements and the weather for many years. Goad, who was also close friends with Ashmole and sent him regular letters detailing astrometerological patterns, had begun his observations nearly two decades earlier, in 1652, and had presented them at a Royal Society meeting. Childrey (who had died in recent months) had also corresponded with the Royal Society.

Childrey, in particular, had been a firm believer in the need to reform astrology and improve its accuracy. 'Were it rectified, it might easily be justified,' he wrote in his book *Britannia Baconia* (1660). 'Now that is partly my aim ... to lay a foundation for the rectifying it ... That there is such a science as astrology, there is no question to be made. The stars have an influence on us ... There is much to be found out, if men did but well attend to observation ...'

Childrey, Gadbury and their circle all thought of themselves as following in the footsteps of Francis Bacon (1561–1626) – England's 'father of modern science'. Bacon's vision of scientific research was threefold: it should consist of data collection on a grand scale (followed by a process of reasoning to produce a theory explaining the observations recorded – the inductive approach), it should be a collaborative affair, and it should have practical applications for the benefit of humankind. Bacon had argued in *New Atlantis* (1626) that such a consensus approach to knowledge, if properly organized and conducted, could increase the power of the English state.

It was because of Bacon, who had reported a Dutch belief that the weather moved in a cycle of around 35 years, that Gadbury had begun his own daily meterological observations (eventually proposing Saturn as the prime mover behind cyclical plague outbreaks). Childrey had been similarly influenced, declaring in a letter to Henry Oldenburg, secretary of the Royal Society: 'I first fell in love with Lord Bacon's philosophy in ye year 1646.'

After the restoration of Charles II, it was Bacon's thinking about the experimental method and the utility of knowledge that was inspiring the astrology profession (as well as members of the Royal Society). Gadbury foresaw a role for the star science in ascertaining which men should be allowed to study at Oxford and Cambridge Universities – only those 'whose genitures render them capable of learning what they ... teach' should be admitted, he thought. Aubrey concurred, commenting that genethlialogy was 'the best guide to direct us to what professions (or callings) children are by nature most fit, or most enclined to'.

Gadbury was also intrigued by the possibility of a passage through northern waters to Asia that would open up commercial shipping routes. His view was that it would take a conjunction of all planets in a northern sign of the zodiac to clear a channel through the ice at the Arctic pole. He even proposed that natal analysis could halt wars. He felt that if more attention had been given to the key players in the recent civil turmoil, then 'much of the misery this nation, during its civil wars underwent, might (by such a knowledge) have been prevented'.

In recent years, such astral projects for the benefit of humankind had been on the increase. Richard Saunders speculated that astrology could be of benefit to eugenics: the quality of the human race could be improved, he theorized, if attention was paid to the position of the planets at conception; 'we might possibly find such heroic spirits and famous worthies of valour and learning in the world as past ages have produced.' Royal Society man William Petty advocated setting up a teaching and research centre to ascertain planetary influences on weather, agriculture and disease (he was another who avidly collated stellar data on the weather, crop fertility and animal and human illnesses).

Francis Bernard wrote to Lilly describing his theory of how to forecast city fires by establishing the founding chart for a particular metropolis from a consideration of the momentous events in its history. 'Time only will show us whether we may direct the fate of cities as of men,' he enthused. Before his death, John Booker too got involved – joining forces with almanac compiler and mathematician Henry Phillippes to consider how to predict tidal patterns.

Lilly had spent some time during the second half of the 1650s making astrometereological observations, and had included some notes in his 1656 *Anglicus*, but had not committed to these ideas. Neither was he enthusiastic about the prospects of the Royal Society men; 'Oh coleworts [kale] and bacon, there's more virtue in that dish, than all the virtuosi [Royal Society men] discover', was his view.

His interests had always tended towards the personal and the prophetic: the majority of his astrological life had been about working with clients using horary to predict the path of good fortune for them. But horary was conspicuous by its absence in Gadbury's almanac.

Lilly knew that Gadbury was disapproving about the more magical and divinatory side of astrology. The younger man had criticized his publication in 1645 of a collection of old prophecies: such soothsaying, Gadbury said, was 'fit only for laughter', and printing it damaged astrology. In his opinion, it was because of 'the apocryphal part of astrology that the sound part so extremely suffers'.

He poured scorn on those who used magical sigils and who resorted to 'a crystal and other pretended cheats and shifts to gull the sillier sort of people'. 'The true astrologer,' he said, 'abominates all such gypsy-like shifts … and thereby frees his science from scandal.'

Gadbury's concern was that astrology's prophetic side was dragging the art down in uncertain, superstitious mud when it could be an experimental and consensual science with the intellectual kudos currently reserved for the new science. 'One real experiment,' he wrote, 'is of greater worth and more to be valued than one hundred pompous predictions.' (In later years, he would admit: 'My inclinations aim at a certainty in science.')

His disparaging view of divinatory astrology resonated, perhaps conveniently, with the ruling elite's attempts to neuter the prognostic side of astrology via strict press censorship. His perspective also chimed with that espoused publicly (but not necessarily privately) by the nation's intelligentsia.

However, his stance was hypocritical and unrealistic. If his grand scheme for repositioning the star science did include abandoning the mantic art's predictive heart, then his research programme would be severely diminished – the majority of its research areas relied on forecasts. His business would disappear too; he himself acknowledged of predictions that 'an almanac without them (like a gentleman money-less) is not regarded'.

Shaking his head, Lilly let Gadbury's pamphlet fall from his hands. Then he turned to pick up his two most recent editions of *Anglicus*. They showed just how the Restoration government viewed predictive astrology – Elias had 'promised assistance to get *Anglicus* licensed by a more learned hand than Crackfarts', but had not yet been successful, and Lilly's publications were still censored severely.

Last year, although he had predicted benignly that 'quietness, peace and tranquillity shall be in all or most nations of Europe', he had run into problems when he highlighted that a planetary movement in 1670 (Saturn entering Pisces) had last occurred in 1641. L'Estrange had allowed him to remind his readers that this was when 'many different judgements in matters appertaining to religion, contrary unto all men's expectation, did then arise and manifest themselves', but had removed the rest of his prophecy, which spoke of religious discord.

Lilly was right to fear that Saturn in Pisces would not bring news of tolerance and amity regarding religion. In April 1670, the government passed the 'Act to prevent and suppress seditious conventicles'. This introduced markedly stiffer fines for preaching at or holding a conventicle (a meeting of any religion other than Church of England). In addition, it removed religious non-conformists' rights to a trial by jury. In William's opinion, the Act was 'the worst ever done'.

He had also been heavily censored (nine lines were expunged from his original manuscript) for suggesting what the earthquakes in Sicily and the subsequent volcanic eruption of Mount Etna in March 1669 portended. A forecast about the downfall of kings and tyrants was removed, as were comments about the demise of Spain's young and infirm monarch, Charles II. L'Estrange, though, had been happy to admit predictions of war and bloodshed for 'the Turks, Tartars, and such like tyrannical people'.

Reluctantly, Lilly started to adopt a more meek and conciliatory tone. He had introduced this year's almanac by saying, 'Having many considerable passages obliterated in our last *Anglicus* of 1670, we must now take care to avoid that rock'. He also stressed that 'The accidents of this year 1671 do not appear in astrology to be written in characters of blood as unto the English ... we have great hopes that the vernal figure [the Sun's ingress into Aries] denotes tranquillity and peace.'

However, he refused to allow his art to be silenced or denied completely, and had included a prediction of troubles ahead for England. From September, he forecast, there would be a move towards 'war and wrangling, or some conspiracies against the lives of mankind'. This was because the figure of heaven for the moment the Sun moved into the sign of Libra at the start of autumn had warmongering Mars and the malefic Dragon's Tail positioned close to the Ascendant.

This carefully worded and brief prognostication escaped the censor. But the difference between what he had been able to say at the start of his career and now was vast – and dispiriting. He could feel his bile rising at Gadbury's very public turning away from horary and his ill-concealed bid to lead the profession. He did not want to see Gadbury at the helm; he did not want astrology to be pulled apart. He had to do something.

Knowing what he did about his former pupil, he would find a

way. Gadbury was his own worst enemy: if he could be provoked into responding in anger, who knew what harm he would do to himself in the process? During their first public spat, Lilly had announced that a collection of nativities to rival Gadbury's was in the press; the book in question was a fiction, but it had the effect of annoying the younger man immensely. What could he do this time?

Resolved to take action, he put his astral literature aside. It was time to take a look at this week's *Gazette*, and perhaps the latest issue of the Royal Society's journal, *Philosophical Transactions*. After that he would read his correspondence. He hoped there would be a letter from Elias – that always raised his spirits.

* * * *

Lilly was shivering. It was December 1673 and it was almost too cold to write. But he wanted to send this letter to Ashmole today. He corresponded regularly – in recent months often two or three times a week, regaling Elias with his professional and domestic affairs, his letters witty, informal and often playful.

He enjoyed signing off according to his current mood and circumstances: 'from your old friend cold William', 'your loving friend W. Anglicus', 'I am old – your old friend, old Anglicus', 'your old loving friend William Senex', and, when he was feeling particularly combative, 'William Wranglicus'.

Missives began in a similar manner. He addressed his successful and affluent friend as: 'My Alexandrine Mecaenas'; 'Honoratissime Patrone', 'My very noble Patron', 'Erudite Patrone' and 'Amicissime Patrone'. A few weeks earlier, it had been 'Patrone Nobilissimme son of God Bacchus'. Then he had had some fun by teasing Elias about his many social engagements – 'I perceive you were the son of Bacchus and Venus, by your so frequent invitations, banquets etc. its well I have the son of a God for my patron.' He had ended that letter exhorting: 'take heed I pray you, that your corpusculum get not a surfett by your jollitys, and frolliqs.'

Often commenting facetiously on his own 'country news', Lilly talked about his servants Henry Rogerson, Mollo, Gabriel and Susan the maid, plus the cat Tab and Ginny the dog, and provided Elias with updates on life outside the capital. There were floods – 'the waters are so high we cannot get to mill with corn, or can the mills work', dinner parties at home with apothecarist and surgeon Thomas Agar, a feud with Justice Matthew Andrews of Hersham after the latter had announced William to be 'a rogue and rascally traitor', and invitations to dine with local resident Frances, Duchess of Somerset.

An encounter with the infamous highwayman Humble Ashenhurst occasioned several letters. Lilly and a neighbour had discovered four suspicious men asleep with their horses in an orchard in the village, and alerted the local constable and the justice of the peace and his men. Together, they apprehended the four men, but in the commotion the ringleader, Ashenhurst, was shot in the back leaving a wound 'one finger deep', two of the men ran off and the fourth, the notorious robber Berkenhead, was arrested and committed to prison but managed to escape.

Lilly accompanied the wounded Ashenhurst to nearby Walton-upon-Thames and tended to him – ordering him a cordial that evening as well as a clyster (enema). He had recognized the thief, recalling that he had seen him pass by his house several times. He quizzed Ashenhurst on this, but the brigand denied he had intentions on William's home: Lilly was old, he had heard, 'but a lusty old man'. Three days after the shooting, Ashenhurst was sent to prison but died within hours of arriving.

As a token of his involvement, William was given one of the firearms used and had relished cautioning Ashmole with it: 'I have just now one of the thieves' pistols given me, Doctor beware of my fury.' (The title Doctor was a reference to Elias's having recently being presented with the degree of 'Doctor of Physick' from the University of Oxford.)

Lilly's continued regard for his stalwart friend shone through his letters. 'Elias,' he said, 'your name is famous, and I do believe your heart is cordial to man.' When the busier of the two had not written for a while, he grumbled: 'I beg humbly, heartily, earnestly for a letter once a fortnight.' But he was not averse to criticizing him – admonishing him, for example, 'to leave swearing, the worst vice you have'.

Their bond had deepened in recent years, in part because of Ashmole's new wife Elizabeth Dugdale (the couple had married on 3 November 1668, seven months after the 70-year-old Lady Manwaring had died). Elizabeth, who was the daughter of one of Ashmole's friends, was now in her early forties – a similar age to Ruth Lilly – and the two couples got along famously. The Lillys joined the Ashmoles in Sheer-Lane near Lincoln's Inn Fields when they went up to London; and the Ashmoles visited Hersham frequently – during the summer they stayed for several weeks or months, as well as enjoying Christmas there.

William had great fun teasing Elias about the close relationship between the new Mrs Ashmole and himself. Referring to Elizabeth as 'my Gallant' and himself as 'her Gallant', he pretended to invite Elizabeth but not her spouse to Hersham: 'she needs not bring her Esquire with her, her Gallant being so lively, – yet if he come my Quaker [Ruth] will entertain him.'

'I wish her health, it's no matter for yours,' he added, declaring: 'I dare not write my own desires to see her, lest Orlando Furioso shall fight me.' Ashmole, he mocked, 'must needs get one pair of yellow stockings' – meaning, in the parlance of the day, that the younger man was a cuckold.

But amidst the jollity, the Lillys provided support for their friends through anguished times. The Ashmoles had been trying to have a baby since the start of their marriage but Elizabeth's pregnancies had so far ended in miscarriage or stillbirth. 'I am sorry my Gallant hath lost all her birds,' William wrote in October 1671; 'get her with child presently,' he urged a month later.

After each tragedy the Lillys opened up their home to their friends: 'I am confident nothing would so recover my poor Gallant as Hersham air, and the sight of her Gallant,' Lilly promised in April 1671. 'My wife is the best nurse of this world.' The Ashmoles' situation was made more poignant by the fact that Elias's first child, from his first marriage when he was 20, had been stillborn; the first Mrs Ashmole had then died suddenly, a year later, while pregnant again. The Lillys, too, had been unable to have children.

Baskets and hampers of food and drink, as well as words, flowed backwards and forwards regularly between the two households. From Hersham came the products of the land Lilly owned (some of which was farmed). Pears, permaines (apples), peaches, 'our grapes', rhubarb, 'our best apples', sacks of wheat and rye, 'half one basket of oatmeal', wooden tubs filled with butter, 'our porke-puddings', a young pig, herbs − betony, sage and chamomile flowers, metheglin (mead flavoured with herbs and spices), six bottles of cider, and cabbages − 'if you will have 2 of our frost bitten cabbages, send word,' Lilly joked. 'I think I heard you say you loved them best of all.'

From London came cloth for new shirts, a large, warm cloak for the master of the house 'of excellent stuff, very complete, well composed both for summer and winter', a coat for Mrs Lilly, calico, Holland cloth, a gown (which fitted very well) and a safeguard (an outer skirt or petticoat).

There was a pound of tobacco when needed for William, ink and paper, soap, six bottles of claret, glasses, 12 bottles of Spanish wine, bees and 'excellent' Cheshire ale, which caused Lilly to salute: 'And, now, a good health, to my patron and Gallant – of Cheshire Ale, which is nappy, good, strong, nutritive, cordial – and God be thanked – nobody loves it but my self.'

The cloak the Ashmoles sent was well used by Lilly. Since leaving London, he had begun studying medicine and in October 1670 he was granted a medical licence from the London College of Physicians. (Ashmole helped him acquire his licence by approaching Dr Sheldon, the Archbishop of Canterbury, on his behalf.) He now rode every Saturday, wrapped in his cloak, to neighbouring Kingston-on-Thames to treat the sick and ailing with a mixture of stellar science and physic.

He was a popular and successful doctor whose skills and charity, according to Ashmole, 'gained him extraordinary credit and estimation'. His friend would later record how 'the poorer sort flocked to him from several parts, and received much benefit by his advice and prescriptions, which he gave them freely, and without money: From those that were more able, he now and then received a shilling, and sometimes a half-crown, if they offered it to him, otherwise he demanded nothing.'

When needed, Lilly prescribed remedies for Ashmole and his family. On this cold December day in 1673, he was concerned about Elizabeth's 'vexatious cough' and wished to advise her what to take – hence the urgency in completing his letter. 'What if she took a pill at night to carry the humour downwards,' he wrote. His suggestion was to combine Jalap, an imported purgative (to carry the humour down), with 'an imperial pill' in the proportions eight grains to two grains, respectively, to create two pills. (An imperial pill was a standard medication which contained the purgatives aloes, agarick, rhubarb and senna, corrected with the aromatics cinnamon, ginger, cloves and nutmeg, with the addition of gum mastic and spikenard, all made into a mass with syrup of violets.)

Elizabeth, he recommended, should take the pills 'in the pap of an apple' (either stewed apple or, if raw, mashed apple) at about four or five o'clock in the morning, and keep in her bed till they worked. Or, if preferred, she could, while fasting, take six grains of Jalap in a posset drink thickened with syrup of maidenhair (two grains), Gycinitis syrup, and a lohoch (a mixture thicker than a syrup) of pinenuts. This concoction should be stirred 'with a liquorice stick' and the sticky mixture licked off when required 'day or night'.

It continued to be a difficult time for the Ashmoles. Elizabeth had terrible toothache, as well as her troublesome cough, and was still trying to conceive and carry a child. An old friend, Dr Thomas Wharton, had just died (the Lillys sent two bottles of metheglin and their pork-puddings to comfort the Ashmoles), and Elias was worried about money too.

He had recently asked Lilly to help him analyze a horary he had cast at 11am on 12 October, asking: 'I have a considerable sum of money lies at interest in the Excise Office: whether I had best let it lie so still, or turn it into gold, & keep it by me'. 'You fear more than you need,' William wrote back; his judgement was that it was good for the money to remain where it was.

He noted that in the horary figure the fixed and stable sign of Capricorn was on the cusp of the second house of resources; the fortunate Dragon's Head was also in this house, and the Part of Fortune was in a fixed sign too – all indicating the money would come to no harm in its present situation at the Excise Office. However, with the Lord of the second house, Saturn, retrograde, he cautioned that if the money was in Ashmole's hands, he 'would either squander it away – or convert it to less purpose – than it is now'.

Elias's concerns also included his work as astrological adviser to Charles II and his court (which Lilly had been helping him with when asked). But the current political climate had resulted in various setbacks for Ashmole. In early 1672, England had finally aligned with Catholic France against Protestant Holland in the third Anglo-Dutch war (Charles had hoped that fighting would begin the year before but had been forced to wait).

However, this decision to ally with the strongest power in Europe (from whom Charles II was receiving secret subsidies) heightened the political and religious tensions re-surfacing in England. There was a growing feeling that the King's foreign and domestic policies were designed to promote Catholicism, which in England was then a much maligned and feared minority faith.

At home there was the very real risk that Charles's successor to the throne would be his Catholic younger brother James, Duke of York. In addition, in March 1672, Charles had issued the Declaration of Indulgence to Dissenters, which allowed non-conformists and Catholics to worship freely and openly, but to many folk looked like their monarch enabling popery to flourish. Within Parliament, members were coming together to oppose the way the King and his government were managing the country's interests.

At the start of this year (1673), as the King prepared to ask the increasingly unhappy Members of Parliament for more money for the seemingly pro-Catholic war, Ashmole had been approached to provide astrological guidance on the situation. In January, he sat down with the Lord Treasurer, Thomas Clifford, one of the leading ministers and a chief promoter of the Declaration of Indulgence. Clifford wanted the following horary answered: 'Whether his Majesty's Declaration of Indulgence of the 15 March 1672 will not occasion such a contest in the House of Commons at their next meeting as to hinder the King's supplies of moneys, unless it be set aside.'

Ashmole's judgement of the horary, cast for 8.15pm on 15 January 1673, was that there were problems ahead for Charles. In his report, he forecast: 'The generality of the House of Commons at their meeting will show themselves averse to the said declaration & use their endeavours to set it aside: insomuch that about the middle of February, the contest relating to the episcopal party and those that are indulged, will grow high, & troublesome; and matters of religion, laws & privileges stoutly stood upon and contended for ... The King will be supplied by the Parliament and about the middle of March the Commons will fall seriously to work about raising of money (though this affair seems a little before to have been impeded) ...'

His prediction proved accurate. Although the Commons did vote to supply the King with £70,000 per month for eighteen months, it delayed passing the bill until the second half of March. Moreover, in order to receive his monies, Charles was forced (after many heated debates in mid-February) to withdraw his Declaration of Indulgence and make a further concession to 'the episcopal party' by agreeing to the introduction of the Test Acts, which barred Catholics and dissenters from holding public office.

Subsequent predictions, though, proved less successful. At the beginning of November, the King called the Commons again to ask for increased war subsidies, and Ashmole was asked to forecast how matters would go between the King and his Parliament (Lilly reminded his friend to 'take notice what time his Majesty makes his speech').

This time, Elias let his judgement be clouded by his sympathies for the King. In both his analysis of Charles II's speech to the House and a horary asked on the topic by Robert Howard, secretary to the Treasury commissioners, he stated that he did not foresee problems ahead.

Regarding the King's speech on 27 October 1673 at 10.50am, he predicted boldly: '... there will be a notable harmony & unity between the King and Parliament within a few days ... the King will be able to dispose of and control the House of Commons in all things

… nor will they be able to carry on any thing if he contradict it … he will have a considerable supply … religion privileges prophets will be settled as he likes … he will now [enter] into better esteem with the Parliament than he lately was.'

That did not happen. The King did not meet with success and was forced to adjourn Parliament repeatedly, but to no avail; the Commons was now prorogued until January next year. When Ashmole turned to him for help, Lilly pointed out that his friend had made a key error in his astrological reasoning – 'you mistake the Significator of the King,' he said. Also, he reminded Elias, malefic Saturn was now in Aries, the zodiac sign associated with England. This did not augur good times for the country.

Ashmole was now waiting anxiously until the New Year, when he would once again assiduously correlate the events in Parliament with the astrological constellations. However, in recent days he had had another upset. Lord Clifford, who had been forced to resign from his post as Lord Treasurer after the Test Acts were passed, had been found dead in a pool of blood – the rumour was that he had committed suicide.

Knowing all this, Lilly was keen to help the Ashmoles in whatever way he could. In his next letter, he thought, he would urge them again to come down to Hersham for Christmas – there was little Elias could do over the festive period, as the Commons would not meet until 7 January.

He also wanted to thank Ashmole for the favours he had done for him in the last month regarding the latest edition of his almanac – without Elias's intervention, he knew he could have been found taking up 'quarters in the Tower, Newgate or Gatehouses'. In addition, there was the matter of securing his successor: Elias had recently put his part in the scheme into motion, and William was impatient to know precisely what had happened. But now, as the December chill settled further into his bones, it was time to finish today's letter, which he did. 'Your old friend young William,' he signed off with a flourish.

* * * *

William and Elias sat across from each other in silence, their eyes fixed on the board placed on the table between them, their expressions eloquent of single-minded resolve: both were determined to win. It was early evening on Monday 7 September 1674 and the last night of the Ashmoles' nearly five-months-long stay in Hersham. Tomorrow Elias and Elizabeth would return to their London life, but tonight was about who would be victorious at *Ludus astrologorum* – the astrologers' game.

The board they were gazing intently at was three feet in diameter, circular and marked with 360 degrees. The design was similar to a circular scheme of heaven, with the twelve signs of the zodiac displayed along a track around the edge of the circle. However, as this was a game for two players, there was another zodiac track positioned within the first (and in opposition to it, so that zodiac signs in the different tracks were aligned with their opposite number, such as Aries with Libra).

The two men were taking it in turns to move their seven counters – representing the Sun, Moon, Mercury, Venus, Mars, Jupiter and Saturn – around the board with the aim of seizing their opponent's Sun, whose loss marked the end of the game. Planning a solar capture was complex, though, and the game typically took hours to play.

The planetary pieces could only progress around the board according to the actual movements of the heavenly bodies (as understood by Ptolemy). This meant that the Sun had to travel forwards around the board, for example, by one degree at a time; the

Moon by a regularly ascending and descending amount (between 12 to 15 degrees) mimicking its apparently faster and slower movement at various times during the month.

Captures were attempted by moving your planetary counter into an allowed astrological aspect (conjunction, square, sextile, trine or opposition) with one of your opponent's pieces, but were only successful if one piece was so strong that it could completely overpower the other. The strengths of the planets involved in each battle were calculated by their position in the heavens: five points (or dignities) were awarded if a planet was in its own house, such as the Sun in Leo or the Moon in Cancer; four points if a planet was in the sign of its exaltation (the Sun in Aries or the Moon in Taurus); fewer points for other positions of strength, including triplicity, term and face.

The outcome of winning a battle was for that planetary counter to increase its power by taking points off the loser; how many points were awarded was determined by the relative strengths of the planets involved in the encounter. For example, if the relative strengths were five points to four points, the victor would emerge with six points, the opponent with three. A capture occurred if a planetary counter was stripped of all of its power in a battle.

William and Elias had been playing the game all summer. At the start of their evening sessions, Lilly won repeatedly – he was still the more learned magus. A disgruntled Elias suggested they mark on the board the locations in which planets enjoyed their various levels of power in order to help him plan his attacks. Lilly disagreed.

However, playing nearly every night had had a marked effect on Ashmole's prowess. The astrologers' game had originally been devised to help undergraduates at universities in England master the intricacies of the mantic art (a similar educational aid existed in Spain), and this had worked for Elias too. Tonight he was close to capturing William's Sun.

Ashmole was thrilled to sight victory but his joy was tinged with concern. He had improved at *Ludus astrologorum*, but he was aware that his friend's poor health was taking a toll. William, who was usually of a strong constitution, had fallen ill of 'a violent humour' a few weeks ago on 26 August – red spots had appeared all over his body, and he also experienced an itching and 'little pushes in his head'.

Lilly thought his distemper might be 'partly scorbutical' (related to scurvy), or a general infection of his blood. So far he had taken some antiscorbutical medicines, such as garden scurvy grass. If his symptoms did not subside soon, he was planning to apply leeches to his haemorrhoids and to open a vein to bleed himself.

His illness changed the tenor of the two men's time together. Their discussions took on a new depth, sometimes a new urgency. Lilly had completed his autobiography for Ashmole in 1667. Now Elias was keen to have answers to the outstanding questions, many of which focused on William's more occult activities, including scrying and conferences with spirits.

Could he say who had been with him 'when he invoked the Queen of Fairies in the Hurst Wood, and upon her appearance was so frighted that he was glad to desist'? Would he say more about what he knew of Dr John Dee's speculator (spirit medium), Edward Kelly? 'What were the reasons why the Angels were not obedient or did not willing[ly] declare their answers to Kelly's questions'?

Ashmole continued to be fascinated by magic and in particular by Dee (to whom his copy of the astrologers' game had belonged). Two summers ago, as part of his project to record the nation's history of astrology, magic and alchemy, he had succeeded in recovering the renowned magician's lost manuscripts and papers, and had had them delivered to Hersham. (They included notes of Dee's conversations with various angels, plus his book describing the invocations or calls to make to summon spirits.)

Last year, while staying with Lilly, he had taken the opportunity to visit Dee's former home in nearby Mortlake and speak with people who had known him. A month ago he had finished transcribing Dee's five *Libri mysteriorum* (describing Dee's angelic magic).

In between their sessions of *Ludus astrologorum*, Elias encouraged William to talk again about his early adventures in the dark arts – how he had studied the grimoire, the *Ars Notoria*, in his early thirties to improve his astrological acumen, and the characters he knew then. Yes, William confirmed, he had known the speculatrix Sarah Skelhorn very well; she had used a crystal to commune with spirits and, in his opinion, 'had a perfect sight ... the best eyes for that purpose I ever yet did see'.

Yes, his former tutor Evans had been asked to perform an invocation by Lord Bothwell and Sir Kenelm Digby (one of the founding members of the Royal Society). However, in this instance, Evans had angered the spirit world by forgetting to perform the necessary suffumigation and, according to him, had been whisked away by the vexed daemon.

Ashmole, in turn, told Lilly about his plans for his ever-growing collection of esoteric and natural curiosities, which now included the rarities of John Tradescant (senior and junior). (Elias had known John Tradescant junior since 1652, when he prepared a catalogue for the 'Tradescants' Ark' – their collection of zoological, mineralogical, ethnological and botanical specimens.)

He had also acquired the late John Booker's manuscripts, as well as those of Simon Forman and the Reverend Richard Napier. Lilly had given him a trunk full of talismans – 'the greatest arcanas any private person in Europe hath' (which had belonged to the aforementioned Lord Bothwell). In the future, Ashmole hoped to be able to preserve Lilly's papers and casebooks too.

His plan, he explained, was to find a way of keeping his vast array of manuscripts and curios together so that the items could be appreciated for many years to come. One idea he had was to approach the University of Oxford: if he bequeathed his collection to academia, would the university erect a large building, suitably aired, to house them? How best should such a collection be administered? Ashmole had strong feelings that it should be open regularly to the public.

Both men talked heatedly and at length about astrology's waning public reputation and the reasons for this. Being silenced by press censorship was one factor, but there were others. Since the Restoration, satire had flourished – nurtured by its ability to transpose displays of anger (which were unwanted in the new regime) into a jocular and partisan art form. Satirical targets were often those groups who had played a role in the years of political and religious turmoil – the radical sects, rabid Presbyterians and ranting astrologers.

The character of the pseudo-astrologer Sidrophel in Samuel Butler's poem *Hudibras* (1662) was a parody of Lilly; John Philips's production *Montelion* (1660) ridiculed him and other astrologers; and the popular drama *The Cheats* (1662) by John Wilson included caricatures of the fraudulent astrologer Mopus and non-conformist minister Scruple. In the play *An Evening's Love: or, The Mock Astrologer* (1671), John Dryden (who was an aficionado in private) indulged in public mockery:

> This, Gallants, we like Lilly can foresee,
> But if you ask us what our doom will be,
> We by tomorrow will our fortune cast,
> As he tells all things when the year is past.

The whole profession was mocked in sham or burlesque pamphlets. *Poor Robin's Almanac*, which was first published in 1662, was the most successful, with sales of around 7,000 a year. It amused its audience with declarations such as, 'every word in this almanac was writ to get money'; or comments to the effect that the physicians were all busy 'killing sick people'; or its lewd prediction that in the spring 'The blood beginneth now to rise, Which makes some maids to scratch their thighs.'

Spoof almanac *Montelion* poked fun at the tendency for compilers to include scientific and mathematical information, such as make-your-own quadrants and astrolabes (readers were expected to cut out the shapes and stick them to a board). Its 1662 edition contained instructions for how to tell the time from the shadow cast by a sundial – but this scientific instrument consisted of a stick stuck up the anus of a bent-over labourer.

Satirical assaults on astrology were not new – the first absurd almanac, *A Mery Prognostication*, had been published in England in 1544. But the current trend to mock the star science and its practitioners coincided with a change that was occurring in the social structure of the nation. In the post-Restoration world, a novel and profound cultural divide was appearing between the patrician classes – the 'better sort' or more respectable people (which included the aristocracy, gentry and the new middle classes) – and the plebeians – the 'vulgar' or labouring folk.

One way for the patrician sort to create a separate, superior identity was to highlight the difference between themselves and those who indulged in vulgar amusements. The result was the emergence of a 'polite', genteel or high culture as distinct from a 'popular', vulgar or low culture. As the years progressed, the gap between the two was growing wider.

In this new, bifurcated and increasingly consumerist society, where it was now important for the polite sort to show through their tastes and values how they were different from the plebeian class, there was a greater emphasis on doing the right thing, whether that was reading the appropriate books, discussing civilized topics or buying suitably tasteful possessions. Social snobbery – shaming people into conformity – had arrived.

For most of its history, astrology was the noble art, practised by and for society's elite. But now it was beginning to be categorized as one of the despised, common pastimes – to be treated with public derision by the polite (even if it was still embraced in the privacy of their parlours).

The tag of vulgarity was easily attached: star-gazers increasingly came from the lower classes, had fewer links with the better sort, and continued to be associated with political subversion, discord and enthusiasm – not characteristics gentlefolk displayed. Sidereal publications (along with chapbooks and ballads) were the cheapest available and, as a result, were more likely than others to be read by the vulgar; their equivalent today is the tabloid or gutter press.

The genteel sort were also being tacitly encouraged, by the government's strict censorship policy regarding prophecy, to class astrology as a vulgar art. In this way, the celestial science was also a victim of ideological domination.

Lilly and Ashmole could see sneering at their art becoming fashionable for genteel folk, but continued to believe that astrology's reputation could be repaired. Ashmole hoped that his holdings of arcana could play a role in raising and maintaining its status, and furthermore he had faith in the experimental method espoused by Gadbury. Lilly felt the way forward was to be true to the art and promote and preserve it at every opportunity – he had plans to produce a revised edition of *Christian Astrology*.

Lilly had also decided at the end of last year that his preference was for Henry Coley to lead the profession after him and had asked Ashmole to help him with his plan. Coley, aged 41, was a skilful astrologer, with a thriving London practice in Baldwin's Gardens, near Holborn – Lilly had already entrusted him with seeing his *Anglicus* through the press. However, Henry was a quiet, family man – hence, in recent months, Lilly had requested that Ashmole introduce Coley to his extensive social circle.

Now, in Hersham, Lilly looked over the board to Ashmole and conceded defeat: Elias had finally captured his Sun. He was tired, but before he bid him goodnight he knew there was one more topic they needed to discuss – John Gadbury.

In his 1673 *Anglicus*, William had praised Coley, declaring the latter to be his 'very worthy friend' and a person of 'great judgement and honesty', as well as recommending his book and his astrological services. But in the same publication, he lambasted Gadbury by again reviling the sign of Scorpio. It was, he taunted, 'a sign of falsity, denoting the person to be arrogant, ambitious, ingrateful, a great boaster, liar, lecherous, perjured, given to all manner of vice and lewdness, revengeful, the worst sign of all the zodiack.'

Could Ashmole confirm that Gadbury was planning a response? Lilly had heard rumours that his carefully chosen words had infuriated him. He knew John had a hot temper – would this be his undoing? Despite the pain of losing the game, his tiredness and his continuing ill health, William Wranglicus smiled. An intemperate response from Gadbury could play straight into his hands.

* * * *

Holding aloft effigies of the Pope, the devil and John Gadbury, the monster procession flanked by thousands of torch bearers marched from Moorgate down to Cheapside and then along past the Royal Exchange to Temple Bar. There, the effigies were thrown on a large bonfire; cats trapped inside their burning bellies screamed, as fireworks lit up the night sky and crowds of not less than 'two hundred thousand' celebrated in the city streets.

Lilly, at Hersham, listened in horror as Henry Coley described Gadbury's part in the spectacular Pope-burning demonstration that had taken place days earlier in November 1679. But what of Gadbury now, he asked? Coley told him all he knew: the astrologer had been taken into custody at the start of the month, accused of being involved in the alleged Popish plot of 1678 to murder Charles II and slaughter thousands of Protestants in order to re-establish Catholicism in England. It was said that Gadbury had elected the most auspicious time to kill the King.

When questioned by the Privy Council, Gadbury had admitted that he had been asked to ascertain whether Charles II's death was imminent and if a Catholic would accede to the throne, but he denied plotting to achieve this. However, he was known to harbour papist sympathies: his mother was a Catholic and, as the Council pointed out, in his current almanac he had omitted details of Guy Fawkes's gunpowder plot in the expected list of notable anniversaries.

Charles II had attended the proceedings and added his own sarcastic query: could the astrologer predict which prison he would end up in? 'The Pope's astrologer' had been incarcerated and was still locked up, with the expectation that he would stand trial and be executed. His only chance lay with his friends – perhaps, said Coley, George Wharton, who was now a baronet and Treasurer of the Royal Ordnance, or Ashmole could intervene to obtain his release.

Lilly hoped there would be good news soon – he disliked Gadbury intensely but did not wish his death. His battle with him was over. He had emerged the victor after the younger man had responded lengthily and with vitriol in a pamphlet, *Obsequium Rationabile* (1675) – so much so that Ashmole and others had leapt to Lilly's defence.

The whole affair had shown Gadbury to be the lesser astrologer and no gentleman.

It was the man who was with Lilly today, and who was now a regular visitor to Hersham, who had been crowned his successor. He had appointed Coley three years earlier by announcing to his readership: 'we are now retired ... we leave behind us (to continue what so many years we have carried on for the honour of astrology) that industrious and no less ingenious artist, Mr. Henry Coley, of whom we have very great hopes ...'

Lilly's announcement was forced, in part, by his increasing infirmity. In late December 1674, a humour 'descended from his head by his left side' down through his calf to his toes and left him lame and feverish for five months, with a weeping blister on his eye. Almost a year later, violent vomiting triggered another bout of fever, which persisted for four months, leaving him extremely weakened, 'together with dimness in his eyes'.

From then on, Coley acted 'as his amanuensis to transcribe (from his dictates) his astrological judgements'. Lilly still had some sight left and could write a little, but he had to rely on Coley more and more: from 1675 onwards, the younger man came to Hersham at the beginning of each summer and stayed until the year's edition was completed.

Lilly's hopes to produce an updated *Christian Astrology* had had to be put aside. However, determined to keep advancing his art and aware that many classic sidereal texts were still available only in Latin, he had begun, with help, to 'English' Guido Bonatti's 'Considerations before judgement' and Girolamo Cardano's aphorisms. *Anima Astrologiae*, a translation of both, was published in 1676, complete with a woodcut engraving of Lilly between his revered predecessors.

William continued to correspond with Elias when he was able – his servant Henry Rogerson writing on his behalf when he could not.

In late January 1675, he struggled to add a few sentences to a letter penned by Rogerson. Mrs Ashmole was ill and it seemed likely she would miscarry again; 'we are heartily sorry for her', he wrote.

He remained in good humour, though, about his ailments – signing himself 'Lame William', 'blind William', 'one eyed old William', 'Your old, lame decrepit friend old William', and when he eventually managed to walk again, 'I am no ambler, or trotter, or galloper – but a very poor padder, yet your old friend.'

When feeling up to it, he was as mischievous as ever in his letters – he took delight in relating how his Ruth had intended 'to cozen her maid with purging ale' but had mistakenly drunk it herself 'so that Sunday, she shit abomination at least 7 or 8 times if not more'. But, occasionally, he acknowledged that his sight was reduced to a 'glimmering', admitting 'my eyes permit no more', 'You must pardon me I cannot read what I write', and simply, but movingly, 'my eyes'.

Today, Coley was visiting Lilly to deliver his latest almanac to him, after he and Ashmole had seen it through licensing and the press. It was a proud moment for Lilly: despite his near blindness and the continued threat of prison (he had now been under restraint nine times), he had warned London in his 1678 *Anglicus* to expect to hear 'seditious words, false and dangerous intelligence, thereby to sow the seeds of division' and had then seen his prediction come true as the city was gripped by the lies and intrigue of the Popish plot.

In the pages of his new *Anglicus* that he now held, he had taken the opportunity to remind his readers of his prescience about these events. He hoped he had many more years to show the world that he saw the future; he still had many secrets in the divinatory art to communicate. Right now, he had a forecast he wanted to discuss with Coley: he had prophesised the appearance of a comet next year. The question was: what did it portend?

Epilogue

Elias Ashmole first saw the 'extraordinary' comet on 21 December 1680. Visible across Europe and in America too, the great comet was one of the brightest of the 17th century, 'with a dreadful tail 50 leagues long, streaming out with a livid and pale light'. People were terrified by what it might augur.

Days later, Elias received news that William Lilly had had 'a flux, which had weakened him much' and left him completely blind. Five months after that, he heard that William was seized on his left-hand side by 'the dead palsy'. Elias went to his side as soon as he could.

He arrived in Hersham on 4 June 'but found him beyond hope'. William recognized Elias, but 'spake little, & some of that scarce intelligible; for the palsy began now to seize upon his tongue'. His larynx had swelled, impeding his swallowing and 'his senses began to fail him'.

Elias and Ruth stayed by his side, doing what they could to comfort him: on 8 June 'he lay in a great agony, insomuch that the sweat followed drop after drop, which he bore with wonderful courage and patience (as indeed he did all his sickness) without complaint.' At about three o'clock in the morning of 9 June 'he died, without any show of trouble or pangs; immediately before his breath went from him, he sneezed three times.'

Lilly was buried in the chancel of the Church of St Mary, in Walton-upon-Thames (where he had been church warden), to the left side of the communion table. Ashmole arranged for his grave to be marked by 'a fair black marble stone' on which he had inscribed, 'Lest it fall into oblivion, William Lilly, most excellent astrologer.' And he acquired his papers, which would become part of the holdings of the country's first museum – the Ashmolean.

After Lilly's death, Obadiah Blagrave printed a 56-line-long elegy for him:

> Our prophet's gone; no longer may our ears
> Be charm'd with musick of th'harmonious spheres.
> Let Sun and Moon withdraw, leave gloomy night ...
> He must be gone, the stars had so decreed;
> As he of them, so they of him, had need.
> This message 'twas the blazing comet brought;
> I saw the pale-fac'd star, and seeing thought
> (For we could guess, but only LILLY knew)
> It did some glorious hero's fall foreshow:
> A hero fall'n, whose death, more than a war,
> Or fire, deserv'd a comet ...

The year after Lilly's death (which was also that of George Wharton's), one of Ashmole's friends, the instrument-maker and Royal Society fellow Joseph Moxon, restored the annual Society of Astrologers' meetings. The revival lasted two years, with the second and final Feast of the Society held in February 1683 at the Three Cranes Tavern in Chancery Lane.

Without its former leader and its founding members, the cohesion of the community was crumbling. Gadbury had avoided execution but was now embroiled in another war of words with an up-and-coming, outspoken star-gazer, John Partridge. Henry Coley was an adept astrologer but lacked Lilly's charisma and dynamism.

In February 1685, Charles II died and his Catholic brother James was crowned King of England. Within months, James II's government announced that almanacs would not receive a licence if they included a prognostication section. After protests from the Company of Stationers, the ban on prophecy was relaxed slightly: compilers were allowed to publish predictions as long as these forecasts were not controversial and were not political in nature.

The astrologers had no option but to comply, albeit reluctantly – those who resisted had their offending words removed. John Partridge fled overseas in disgust. In the political sense, almanacs were now completely neutered. The government had finally won the fight to control public prophecies.

At first, sales of almanacs and the numbers of editions produced remained steady, with total sales of around 400,000 and 50 compilers; but by the 1690s the number of authors began to fall – a sign of the loss of vitality in the market.

Barred from prophesying about politics, almanac writers moved to fill their pages with other information: assertions of the astrologers' love for the reigning sovereign, mathematical problems and science. Gadbury took to including details of his astrological research.

At the end of the century, Henry Coley, who had continued his successful practice as a horary astrologer, felt the need to remind his audience that predictions were still part of astrology's craft. In his 1691 almanac, he wrote: 'Now as to the knowledge of future contingencies, I know there are many good people that will not allow or believe it possible to be done by man … yet some things are and may be known by us, or at least modestly hinted at.' In deference to the government's continuing censorship, he added: 'I shall not therefore point at any particular person or nation peremptorily.'

However, his stance was fast becoming outmoded – the majority of astrologers were publicly (at least) turning their backs on the divinatory aspect of their art. This included the new head of the profession, John Partridge, whose book *Opus Reformatum* (1693) disowned the art of horary. His contemporary John Whalley concurred, decrying horary questions as 'Imaginary, un-natural, arbitrary whimsies, like those of geomancy ...'

The new, fashionable ladies' and gentlemen's magazines that appeared at the turn of the century summed up what the polite sort's position should be. The periodical *Ladies' Diary* in 1723 declared that 'there's no such thing as foretelling events'; the *Spectator* of 12 October 1712 told its readers that those who still had time for the star science were lacking in intelligence:

> It is not to be conceived how many wizards, gypsies and cunning men are dispersed through all the counties and market towns of Great Britain, not to mention the fortune-tellers and astrologers, who live very comfortably upon the curiosity of several well-disposed persons in the cities of London and Westminster. Notwithstanding these follies are pretty well worn out of the minds of the wise and learned in the present age, multitudes of weak and ignorant persons are still slaves to them.

Although the words in the *Spectator* reveal that some of the gentry did disregard the cultural hegemony of the day and still appreciated astrology, the art of divination by this time was established decisively in popular public opinion as deviant and dangerous.

Then, in 1736, just over 100 years after Lilly began his extraordinary career, astrology as a whole was outlawed when the

Witchcraft Act of that year made all acts of foreseeing the future illegal, not just recovering lost or stolen goods. The penalty for any form of prediction was one year's imprisonment and being pilloried on market day four times a year.

There were significant cultural messages about astrology and the occult within this legal reform. The Witchcraft Act repealed the previous legislation on the assumption that witchcraft simply did not exist. The wording of the Act, stating that prosecutions would be against anyone pretending to make a judgement about the future, also underlined the idea that in the view of right-minded people all divination was deception.

In addition, this new law against those who 'pretend to exercise or use any kind of witchcraft, sorcery, enchantment, or conjuration, or undertake to tell fortunes …' formed part of the Vagrancy Act. All those who foretold the future, it implied, were likely to be ne'er-do-wells, living from hand to mouth – not educated, intelligent professional folk.

In 1824, the Vagrancy Act was amended, and for the first time made charging money for forecasts an offence. In its language, the Act 'for the punishment of idle and disorderly persons, and rogues and vagabonds' underlined more definitively that astrology was a fraud. Section 4 of the new legislation stated that the statute applied to 'every person pretending or professing to tell fortunes, or using any subtle craft, means, or device, by palmistry or otherwise, to deceive and impose on any of his Majesty's subjects …'

Fortune-telling was placed at the head of a list of misdemeanours likely to be committed by vagrants – in front of such offences as gambling in the street, obscene exposure and carrying a cutlass with the intent to commit a crime. The standard penalty was three months' hard labour or a spell in prison.

In response, the majority of astrologers shifted the public focus of their profession to one of character reading. Analyzing an individual's character or psychology, discussing in general terms tendencies to act in a particular way, meant that prosecution under Section 4 could be avoided.

Predictive astrology disappeared further underground as a new sanitized psychological version full of woolly statements rose up at the end of the 19th century and the start of the next. 'Sun sign astrology', which focuses solely on the position of the Sun in an individual's birth chart, is part of this movement.

By the start of the 1970s, the generally held view of horary astrology was summed up in the textbook *The Compleat Astrologer* (1971) by Derek and Julia Parker, who wrote: 'the notion that the planetary positions can produce an "answer" of this kind, usually to the most petty questions, seems too absurd for consideration ...' (Four years later Derek Parker would publish the first biography of William Lilly.)

Divinatory astrology remained illegal in the UK until 16 November 1989 when Section 4 of the Vagrancy Act was repealed as part of the Stature Law (Repeals) Bill. This legalization of prediction based on the movements of the planets and stars occurred as a resurgence of interest in the art of horary astrology and William Lilly gathered pace. In 1980, an extant copy of the first edition of *Christian Astrology* had been discovered, and this was followed in 1985 by the publication of a new version of it.

Today, the number of astrologers practising horary and other predictive techniques (which are together referred to as traditional astrology) is increasing. Without *Christian Astrology* this would not have been possible. Predictive astrology is also making a dent in public consciousness again. John Frawley, who cites William Lilly as a major influence, has appeared on television in the UK making predictions regarding upcoming sports matches.

One of his many successes was prophesying the outcome of the

1999 football European cup final between Manchester United and Bayern Munich: Frawley's forecast was that the English side would win 2-1. Five minutes before the end of the match, with United facing a 1-0 defeat, it looked like Frawley was wrong, but his pre-match prediction proved correct. Manchester United scored two goals in the final minute of the game.

The waxing appreciation of predictive astrology has seen a shift away from trying to fit the art within the mechanistic cause-and-effect model of modern science, and a swing back to considering astrology as a spiritual discipline. Today, for many astrologers interested in foretelling the future, astrology is divination – communication with the divine – just as it was in the beginning for the Babylonians and in the 17th century for William Lilly.

What remains is for 21st-century society to look again at the mysterious, fascinating conundrum of astrological prediction. The question is: are we broad-minded and brave enough? Or will we continue to sneer because that is what our so-called authority figures tell us to do?

After the upheaval of the English Civil War, it was the country's ruling elite who sought to contain the disruptive power of the sidereal art by promoting a view of astrology as dangerous and not *de rigueur* for polite society. Today it is scientists keen to preserve the stability and order brought by the notion of a mechanistic universe who deride astrology the most vociferously.

But, as this century progresses, what is becoming clearer is our lack of understanding of the material world – highlighted in the realization that ordinary matter accounts for less than five per cent of the universe. With this in mind, looking for answers purely in the material realm, as we know it, is narrow-minded in the extreme.

William Lilly's legacy is to embrace that there is more to this world than the material, and to appreciate that the cosmos is an enchanted place. For those approaching with a pure heart, as Lilly knew well, foreknowledge can be tasted.

Sources and Notes

Elias Ashmole preserved William Lilly's casebooks, almanacs, autobiography and letters. Much of the material in this book is drawn directly from these sources. His casebooks, letters and some almanacs are in the Bodleian Library, in Oxford; other almanacs are in the British Library, in London. Lilly's casebooks can be viewed in the Duke Humfrey reading room at the Bodleian Library. They are:

1644–1645 Ashmole 184

1645–1646 Ashmole 178

1646–1647 Ashmole 185

1647–1648 Ashmole 420

1649 Ashmole 210

1654–1656 Ashmole 427

1661 Ashmole 430

Elias Ashmole published Lilly's autobiography in 1715 as *Mr William Lilly's History of his Life and Times*; Katherine Briggs re-edited and published it in 1974 as *The Last of the Astrologers* (Folklore Society). An electronic copy of a 1772 edition of *Mr William Lilly's History of his Life and Times* is accessible at the Project Gutenburg website, http://gutenberg.org/files/15835/15835-h/15835-h.htm (accessed 27 April 2014).

The early modern texts quoted here have been modernized in order to make the text more accessible to 21st-century readers. This has involved, for example, expanding standard contractions, removing capitalizations and amending spellings, in a manner that tries to maintain a balance between sensitivity to the text and the needs of the modern audience (see *Editing Early Modern Texts: an introduction to principles and practice*, Michael Hunter, Palgrave Macmillan, 2009).

All dates pre-1752 are in the Old Style (OS) Julian calendar, unless indicated as New Style (NS) Gregorian calendar. In Lilly's day, the Julian calendar differed from the Gregorian one by ten days, which means, for example, that Lilly's birthday, 1 May 1602 (OS), is our 11 May 1602 (NS). In addition, in England in Lilly's era, the year changed on 25 March, rather than 1 January as it does today. During March there was a convention to write the date including both years – for example, 9 March 1643/44 for a date which we now designate 9 March 1644. For clarity, all Old Style dates during March in this book have used the modern notation for the year.

The astrological charts were cast using Janus software.

Notes

Introduction, pp.xv–xvi
page xv: 'At exactly 11am on Monday 15 September 2003, a commemorative plaque was unveiled ...' The plaque reads: 'William Lilly (1602–1681) Master Astrologer Lived in a house on this site.' It is placed on the site of the former Strand tube station in Aldwych.

Chapter 1: The Piss-prophet Rises, pp.1–30
page 2: 'Her query "Should I marry?"...' This query and the following ones, up to 'When will my son be home?', were all asked in the early years of the Civil War, but not all on this particular day (Ashmole 184 and 178).

page 3: 'Gaining military insight ...' Lilly discusses these military questions in *Christian Astrology*.

page 6: 'It took Lilly about ten minutes to cast the chart ...' Lilly's analysis of John Pym's urine is in *England's Prophetical Merlin*, 1644.

page 9: 'One of his closest friends was the royalist Sir William Pennington ...' Davy Ramsey introduced William Lilly and William Pennington in 1634. Ramsey and Lilly both attended the treasure-hunting party in Westminster Abbey in 1634. It is not known if Pennington was a member of this treasure-hunting party.

page 10: 'The occasion was a treasure-hunting expedition ...' Lilly describes this event in his autobiography.

page 11: 'Musgrave was charmed by Lilly and ... agreed to join him for a drink.' It is not known on what date during 1643 Lilly helped Pennington to track down the sequestration order, and met Musgrave. Lilly describes their meeting in his autobiography.

page 13: 'almanacs incorporated gossip, health advice ...' Bernard Capp, *Astrology and the Popular Press: English Almanacs 1500–1800* (Faber & Faber, 1979), is an in-depth account of the development of almanacs.

page 14: 'The first emperor of Rome, Augustus ...' The history of astrology is covered in Benson Bobrick, *The Fated Sky: Astrology in History* (Simon & Schuster, 2005), James Herschel Holden, *A History of Horoscopic Astrology* (American Federation of Astrologers, 2006) and Peter Whitfield, *Astrology: A History* (The British Library, 2001).

page 15: 'Duke Galeazzo Maria Sforza ... prediction.' Many thanks to H Darrel Rutkin for telling me about this incident; this and the role of medical and political astrology at court in Renaissance Milan are covered in Monica Azzolini, *The Duke and the Stars* (Harvard University Press, 2013).

page 16: 'Abbott Orazio Morandi ... before his case could come to trial.' Abbott Orazio Morandi's astrological political think-tank is detailed in Brendan Dooley, *Morandi's Last Prophecy and the End of Renaissance Politics* (Princeton University Press, 2002).

page 16: 'In England, regulations to control astrologers ...' The legal situation surrounding astrology is covered in Keith Thomas, *Religion and the Decline of Magic* (Weidenfeld & Nicolson, 1971).

page 17: 'During the 1630s, only one almanac author, John Booker, risked prosecution ...' These events are described in Bernard Capp, *Astrology and the Popular Press: English Almanacs 1500–1800* (Faber & Faber, 1979).

page 23: 'Aiming to discredit the younger, less experienced astrologer ...' Astrology's propaganda role in the Civil War is considered in Harry Rusche, 'Merlini Anglici: Astrology and propaganda from 1644 to 1651', *The English Historical Review*, vol. 80, no. 315 (April 1965), pp322–33.

page 25: '"heretics, robbers, pederasts, sodomites ..."' Anthony Grafton, *Cardano's Cosmos: The worlds and works of a renaissance astrologer* (Harvard University Press, 1999).

page 29: '"this unlucky judgement"...' Lilly discusses this in his autobiography. Bulstrode Whitelocke describes one discussion with Lilly, on 9 June 1645, about 'this unlucky judgement' (Bulstrode Whitelocke, *Memorials of the English Affairs*, 1682). It is not known if Lilly had already advised Whitelocke in late 1644/early 1645 that the New Model Army should hold back from fighting until 10 or 11 June 1645 or later. It is not certain either if Lilly spoke directly to others within his circle of parliamentary and military contacts about 'this unlucky judgement'.

Chapter 2: The Society of Astrologers of London, pp.31–58

page 32: 'the Committee of Examinations ... wanted answers' This episode is related in Lilly's autobiography.

page 36: 'how the position of the Sun in the King's birth chart augured that he was in great danger of a sudden and violent death.' Lilly's royal death prophecies are discussed in detail in Ann Geneva, *Astrology and the Seventeenth-century Mind: William Lilly and the language of the stars* (Manchester University, 1995).

page 40: 'Looking around the room ... Lilly was happy to see so many of his peers.' Lilly, Ashmole, Wharton and Culpeper have all been identified as attending meetings of the Society of Astrologers of London; the identities of other attendees remain uncertain. Further details of the Society's meetings can be found in Patrick Curry, 'The Astrologers' Feasts', *History Today*, vol. 38, issue 4, April 1988, pp17–22.

page 41: '"late stool"' Ashmole's account of his 'late stool' is in his diary. This journal and his correspondence are published in *Elias Ashmole (1617–1692): his autobiographical and historical notes, his correspondence, and other contemporary sources relating to his life and work,* edited by Dr C H Josten (Oxford: Clarendon Press, 1966, 5 vols).

page 42: 'Captain Bubb ... exemplified the rogues within the profession.' Lilly describes the rogues' gallery of London's early 17th-century astrologers and others, including his tutor John Evans, in his autobiography.

page 46: 'Antrobus "had baptized a cock ..."' Lilly describes this episode in his autobiography; he was successful in helping Pennington oust Antrobus from his parsonage.

page 50: 'Current thinking suggested that the birth of Jesus Christ ... on the Pisces-Aries cusp.' It was Geoffrey Cornelius, in his afterword to Lilly's *Christian Astrology* (Regulus, 1985), who put forward the idea that the background of the portrait engraving of Lilly aged 45 depicts the conjunction of Saturn and Jupiter in 7 BCE.

page 52: 'The query was, "If Presbytery shall stand?"...' Differing views about Lilly's judgement on this are given by John Frawley in *Vox Lillii Vox Dei: 'If Presbytry shall stand?'*, accessible at http://www.johnfrawley.com/#!vox-lillii-vox-dei/c1n8r (accessed 30 April 2014) and Geoffrey Cornelius in *The Moment of Astrology: Origins in Divination* (The Wessex Astrologer, 2003).

page 53: 'the magi of the ancient Near East (the *umannu*) held the most important civil job in the realm ...' The role of the *umannu* is explored in depth in Simo Parpola, *Letters from Assyrian and Babylonian Scholars (State Archives of Assyria)* (Helsinki University Press, 1993).

page 53: 'Since medieval times in the Western world ...' The place of astrology at court and the universities in Europe is covered in Hilary M Carey, *Courting Disaster: Astrology at the English Court and University in the Later Middle Ages* (Palgrave Macmillan, 1992), H Darrel Rutkin, 'Astrology' (Chapter 23) in *The Cambridge History of Science* (vol. 3, *Early Modern Science*), edited by Katherine Park and Lorraine Daston (Cambridge University Press, 2006) and Monica Azzolini, *The Duke and the Stars* (Harvard University Press, 2013).

page 57: 'a tall, round-faced, pox-marked and red-haired gentlewoman ...' Lilly describes his encounter with Jane Whorewood in his autobiography.

Chapter 3: The Intelligencer of the Stars, pp.59–84

page 59: 'Look to yourselves, the cannon in the castle is about to be discharged.' Lilly's and Booker's visit to the parliamentarian forces during the besiegement of Colchester is covered in Lilly's autobiography.

page 61: 'plenty to compare and discuss as they headed back to the metropolis.' It is not known what Lilly and Booker discussed on their journey back from Colchester to London.

page 61: '"all manner of drudgeries"' Lilly's account of his early years in London and his first marriage occurs in his autobiography.

page 63: 'the men reassured both the soldiery and General Fairfax ...' Lilly's and Booker's visit to the New Model Army's headquarters in Windsor and Hugh Peter is described by Lilly in his autobiography.

page 65: 'The plan, Whorewood told Lilly, was for the King to escape ...' Lilly's involvement in the King's plans to escape from Carisbrooke Castle is revealed in his autobiography.

page 66: '"Whether by joining with the agents of the private soldiery of the army ..."' The note sent by Richard Overton and the chart Lilly drew up are in the Bodleian Library (Ashmole 420, f267).

page 69: 'Jane Whorewood ... visited Lilly to ask him to elect the most auspicious time ...' This meeting is described in Lilly's autobiography.

page 71: 'For example, when the city of Baghdad ...' The foundation chart of Baghdad is discussed in James H Holden's article at http://cura.free.fr/xxv/25hold3.html (accessed 24 February 2014).

page 75: '"the intelligencer of the stars"' This was how Lilly was described by the newsbook *Mercurius Civicus* in its edition for 29 October 1646; cited in Joad Raymond, *The Invention of the Newspaper: English Newsbooks 1641–1649* (Oxford University Press, 2005).

page 77: 'Now, with his first talk imminent ...' The dates that Lilly gave talks in 1648 and 1649 are not known.

page 79: 'the majority of early omen astrology had centred on eclipses ...' The early days of omen astrology are covered in Simo Parpola, *Letters from Assyrian and Babylonian Scholars (State Archives of Assyria)* (Helsinki University Press, 1993), Francesca Rochberg, *The Heavenly Writing: Divination, Horoscopy, and Astronomy in Mesopotamian Culture* (Cambridge University Press, 2007) and Tamsyn Barton, *Ancient Astrology* (Routledge, 1994).

page 80: '"the Lord of the 10th is eclipsed"' This unpublished manuscript is in the Bodleian Library, Ashmole 240, article 130, f281, and is discussed by Ann Geneva in *Astrology and the seventeenth-century mind: William Lilly and the language of the stars* (Manchester University, 1995).

Chapter 4: 'Ye Famous Mr William Lilly', pp.85–108

page 86: 'Underneath the vermilion cape, the rest of his clothes were just as striking.' Ashmole describes his clothes in wonderful detail in his journal, published in *Elias Ashmole (1617–1692): his autobiographical and historical notes, his correspondence, and other contemporary sources relating to his life and work*, edited by Dr C H Josten (Oxford: Clarendon Press, 1966, 5 vols).

page 86: 'The rift in their friendship had not been entirely unexpected.' Lilly describes Ashmole's betrayal in his autobiography.

page 97: 'William had even misled his public about his nativity.' The details of Lilly's nativity are still disputed. The chart here is based on a chart endorsed by Elias Ashmole, which is in the Bodleian Library (Ashmole 394). It places Lilly's Ascendant at 3 56 Pisces, Sun at 20 4 Taurus, Moon at 15 33 Capricorn and Part of Fortune at 29 25 Libra. John Gadbury published a different nativity for Lilly in his *Collectio Geniturarum* (1662). Sue Ward discusses Lilly's nativity in her article 'Beyond the Great Fire: Lilly and Ashmole', accessible at http://easyweb.easynet.co.uk/~sueward/articles/Beyond%20the%20Great%20Fire.pdf (accessed 30 April 2014).

page 90: 'He wanted Lilly to save George Wharton's life.' Lilly describes his involvement in saving Wharton's life in his autobiography.

page 91: 'My best of friends: If in these worst of times ...' Wharton's invitation in verse to Ashmole is the Bodleian Library (Ashmole 423, f278).

page 93: '"Whether it will be good for me to take the house near Boswell Court."' Elias Ashmole recorded in his journal that he asked Lilly this question on 17 October 1650. On the same day, at 1.30pm, he also recorded that he cast a horary enquiring where his wife's pox talisman was. It is not known if he discussed the pox query with Lilly; nor do we know anything about the nature of their other discussions that day. The pox talisman was found in his wife's chamber pot.

page 95: 'Unusually for William, he was late rising … Elias Ashmole had fallen "ill of a surfett" at 1am.' Elias Ashmole fell 'ill of a surfett' after attending the Society of Astrologers' meeting on Thursday 14 August 1651; it is not known if William Lilly was late rising the next day; nor do we know the identities of the attendees apart from Ashmole. Ashmole did not record any activities in his journal the day after his 'surfett'; he was back in action by the day after that.

page 100: 'Addressing the Society, Culpeper had stressed …' Nicholas Culpeper spoke at the Society about his book *Astrological Judgement of Diseases from the Decumbiture of the Sick.* The precise nature of his talk and the date it was given remain uncertain. Culpeper's comments are from *Astrological Judgement of Diseases from the Decumbiture of the Sick.*

page 107: 'One of the newcomers, 21-year-old John Rowley from Luton …' The letters to Lilly from John Rowley and others, including Richard Napier, Vincent Wing, Abraham Wheelock, the Italian gentleman, and George Wharton's to Bulstrode Whitelocke, are in the Bodleian Library.

page 105: 'There were two letters to open.' The date these letters arrived at the Corner House is not known. 'Ye Famous Mr William Lilly' is in Ashmole 240, f250; 'to the Ptolomy …' in Ashmole 423, f239.

page 106: 'In addition, Nicholas Culpeper was living up to his name …' Culpeper's work is covered in Graeme Tobyn, *Culpeper's Medicine: a practice of Western holistic medicine* (Element Books, 1997).

page 108: 'He had asked Ashmole … Bradfield House, in Berkshire.' Ashmole cast a horary on 22 February 1652 asking if it would be good for him if Lilly came to live at Bradfield House; it is not known what else the men discussed when this move was broached.

Chapter 5: The Dark Year, pp.109–141

page 110: 'The astrologers were on the roof of Southampton House …' The pamphlet *Black Munday Turn'd White* places 'Mr Lillie, Mr Culpeper and the rest of the Society of Astrologers' at 'Southampton house, to take their observation'.

page 110: 'on what had already become known as Black Monday.' William E Burnes's article on Black Monday, *'The terriblest Eclipse That Hath Been Seen in Our days': Black Monday and the Debate on Astrology during the Interregnum,* is published in *Rethinking the Scientific Revolution,* edited by Margaret J Osler (Cambridge University Press, 2000).

page 112: '"heeded more of late with us ... since the creation."' Nathaniel Homes in *Plain Dealing* (1652).

page 119: 'He had set out immediately to meet with the Speaker of the House of Commons, William Lenthall ...' The events around Lilly's experience in front of the Committee for Plundered Ministers are described in his autobiography.

page 128: 'and he had recently bought it and its accompanying land.' Lilly bought his Hersham property in 1652; he stayed there for a period that year, but the dates he did so are unknown.

page 128: 'It was a large house (of 13 hearths) ...' Details of the size of Lilly's Hersham property can be found in Derek Parker, *Familiar to All: William Lilly and astrology in the seventeenth century* (Jonathan Cape, 1975).

page 129: 'There were more than 200 books ...' All the books in Lilly's library of occult manuscripts are listed in *Christian Astrology*; it is not known what sidereal instruments he owned.

page 131: 'The man in question – John Gadbury – was here now on this October day in the study.' Lilly opened up his library to John Gadbury; it is not known if Lilly and Gadbury were there together while Ruth sang downstairs.

page 132: '"Pale and swarthy"' John Gadbury's description of himself is in *Doctrine of Nativities*, 1658.

page 136: 'In July, a young woman, Anne East ...' A copy of the indictment filed against Lilly by East is given in his autobiography.

page 141: 'and doing him "many superlatively-manifest injuries".' John Gadbury included these comments about Lilly in his 1659 pamphlet *The Nativity of the late King Charles*.

Chapter 6: Hieroglyphics of Hell, pp.143–170

page 143: 'Inside Westminster's Gatehouse prison ...' Lilly describes this arrest and incarceration, and being quizzed by Parliament about the identity of Charles I's masked executioner, in his autobiography.

page 148: 'Fifth Monarchist John Spittlehouse ... "the prince of astrologers".' In John Spittlehouse, *Rome Ruin'd by Whitehall* (1650). The connections between astrology and the radicals are discussed in Keith Thomas, *Religion and the Decline of Magic* (Weidenfeld & Nicolson, 1971).

page 149: 'he had been talking about retiring for the last five years.' Lilly first mentioned retirement in his 1656 *Anglicus*.

page 149: 'reading a letter from fellow astrologer Thomas Heydon.' Heydon's letter to Lilly is in the Bodleian Library, Ashmole 423, f242.

page 150: 'Gadbury's complaint at the time ... "both his pen, purse, and person, for, and on his behalf".' John Gadbury, 1659, *The Nativity of the late King Charles*. It is unclear precisely why Gadbury was so offended, and whether Lilly understood what had triggered the original dispute.

page 150: 'Gadbury had published a book, ...' Sue Ward's and Peter Stockinger's article *'Monster of ingratitude'* looks in depth at the argument between Lilly and Gadbury; it is published in *Lilly, The Last Magician* (Oxford: Mandrake of Oxford, 2014).

page 151: 'In October 1662, when John Booker's younger son Samuel ...' This letter is in Ashmole 180, f122.

page 153: 'illustrate, enlarge and refine arts like the tried gold.' *Elias Ashmole (1617–1692): his autobiographical and historical notes, his correspondence, and other contemporary sources relating to his life and work,* edited by Dr C H Josten (Oxford: Clarendon Press, 1966, 5 vols), p136.

page 156: 'In 1658, Sarah Jinner became the first female astrologer ...' *'An Almanack: Or, Prognostication for the Year of Our Lord, 1658'* by Sarah Jinner is in the British Library, London, together with her other editions.

page 158: '"The late years of the tyranny ... to write and teach astrology and physic."' John Heydon in *The Wise-Mans Crown: or, the Glory of the Rosie-Cross* (1664).

page 158: 'However, there was one young man ... and here was a chance to cement their friendship.' Lilly and Coley and their circle of colleagues and acquaintances drank in coffee-houses; the dates of these events, and other details of when and where Lilly and Coley met, are uncertain.

page 158: 'This was "the law near tottering ..."' Lilly explained the meaning of some of the hieroglyphics in his 1655 *Anglicus*.

page 159: 'two of these portentous "enigmatical types" had become notorious ...' Lilly's questioning, by the government, about his involvement in the Great Fire of London is described in his autobiography.

page 167: 'At Ashmole's request, he had recently started writing his autobiography ... John Booker, who was Lilly's age, had died.' Lilly began to write his autobiography some time in 1667, after Elias Ashmole had asked him to do so; it is unclear if Booker's death on 8 April 1667 was the catalyst for this.

page 167: 'So far, Lilly had completed about half of the detailed analysis of Ashmole's birth chart ...' Lilly finished this first part of the analysis of Ashmole's horoscope and directions on 16 October 1667; at Ashmole's request, he had also drawn up the horoscope of the placing of the first stone of the Royal Exchange by

Charles II on 23 October 1667. When or where the two men met to discuss these analyses is unknown.

page 168: 'William was in the city to complete the process of getting his latest almanac printed ...' Lilly finished his 1668 almanac on 27 September 1667; we can only estimate that it was late October when he visited London to complete the process of getting it licensed and through the press.

page 168: ' "old Crackfarts" ... "macerated, obliterated, sliced and quartered." ' Lilly complained about this in a letter to Ashmole on 20 November 1671 (this is in *Elias Ashmole (1617–1692)*.

page 169: 'Old Crackfarts had censored him heavily again ...' Thirteen of Lilly's original manuscripts for the almanacs that L'Estrange censored are in the Bodleian Library, Oxford, MS 353.

page 170: 'That is it, thought Lilly: I will urge Elias to use his influence ...' In a letter to Ashmole dated 1 July 1672, in the Bodleian Library, MS 241, f202, Lilly wrote: 'many thanks for your last letter, for ye promised assistance to get *Anglicus* licensed by a more learned hand, than of Crackfarts.'

Chapter 7: The Last Magus, pp.171–198

page 173: 'Royal Society man John Aubrey ...' John Aubrey's life is detailed in Michael Hunter, *John Aubrey and the Realm of Learning* (Gerald Duckworth, 1975).

page 174: 'Childrey had also been a firm believer in the need to reform astrology and improve its accuracy.' The move to reform astrology and the various projects to do so are covered in Bernard Capp, *Astrology and the Popular Press: English Almanacs 1500–1800* (Faber & Faber, 1979) and Patrick Curry, *Prophecy and Power: Astrology in Early Modern England* (Princeton University Press, 1989).

page 176: 'Oh coleworts and bacon ...' Lilly wrote this in a letter to Elias Ashmole dated 12 January 1671; Lilly's letters to Ashmole are in *Elias Ashmole (1617–1692)*.

page 176: 'Gadbury was disapproving about the more magical and divinatory side of astrology.' 'It is by reason of the apocryphal part of astrology that the sound part so extremely suffers' (Gadbury, 1666); 'The true astrologer abominates all such gypsy-like shifts' (John Gadbury, *The Nativity of King Charles I*, 1659); 'One real experiment is of greater worth and more to be valued than one hundred pompous predictions' (Gadbury, 1665); 'My inclinations aim at a certainty in science' (Gadbury, 1669). Gadbury's rationalism is discussed in Bernard Capp, *Astrology and the Popular Press: English Almanacs 1500–1800* (Faber & Faber, 1979), and

Patrick Curry, *Prophecy and Power: Astrology in Early Modern England* (Princeton University Press, 1989).

page 179: 'the book in question was a fiction ...' Lilly's fictitious book of nativities is mentioned in *Anglicus* 1660.

page 179: 'Lilly was shivering ... almost too cold to write.' Lilly comments on how cold it is are in a letter to Elias Ashmole written on 13 November 1673.

page 180: '"one finger deep"' Lilly's encounter with infamous highwayman Humble Ashenhurst was in July 1670.

page 183-4: 'On this cold December day in 1673 ... advise her what to take – hence the urgency in completing his letter.' Lilly prescribed a remedy for Elizabeth Ashmole's 'vexatious cough' in his letter of 4 December 1673.

page 188: 'but tonight was about who would be victorious at – the astrologers' game.' Ashmole did indeed own a copy of *Ludus astrologorum*, which had belonged previously to John Dee; it is not known if Ashmole and Lilly played the astrologers' game together.

page 188: 'The board they were gazing intently at was three feet in diameter, circular and marked with 360 degrees.' The astrologers' game is discussed in Ann Moyer's paper 'The Astronomers' Game: Astrology and University Culture in the Fifteenth and Sixteenth Centuries', *Early Science and Medicine*, vol. 4, no. 3, 1999, pp228–50.

page 190: 'Could he say who had been with him ...' Ashmole asked Lilly these additional questions about his autobiography, concerning the Queen of Fairies and other topics; but it is not known precisely when.

page 191: 'In between their sessions of ...' The Ashmoles lived with the Lillys for nearly five months in 1674 (between April and September); it is uncertain what the men talked about during this time.

page 192: 'Both men talked heatedly and at length about astrology's waning public reputation and the reasons for this.' It is not certain how Lilly and Ashmole felt about astrology's changing status.

page 195: 'hence, in recent months, Lilly had requested that Ashmole introduce Coley to his extensive social circle.' Lilly asked Ashmole to introduce Coley to his social circle in his letter of 16 October 1673; this may or may not have been part of a plan by Lilly to help establish Coley as his successor.

page 197: '"we are now retired ..."' Lilly's 1676 *Anglicus*.

Epilogue, pp.199–206

page 202: 'Then, in 1736 ... astrology as a whole was outlawed ...' The legal situation surrounding astrology during the 18th, 19th and 20th centuries is discussed in Owen Davies, *Witchcraft, Magic and Culture 1736–1951* (Manchester University Press, 1999); Owen Davies, 'Decriminalising the witch: the origin of and response to the 1736 Witchcraft Act' in John Newton and Jo Bath (eds), *Witchcraft and the Act of 1604* (Brill, 2008); Maureen Perkins, *The Reform of Time: Magic and Modernity* (Pluto Press, 2001); and Patrick Curry, *A Confusion of Prophets: Victorian and Edwardian Astrology* (Collins & Brown, 1992).

page 204: **'By the start of the 1970s, the generally held view of horary astrology ...'** The view of horary during the 20th century and the revival of what is now known as traditional astrology are discussed in Deborah Houlding's article 'Prediction, Providence & the Power of the "Self" in Horary' which is available at *http://www.skyscript.co.uk/horary_prediction.html* (accessed 9 May 2014); in Nicholas Campion's, 'The Traditional Revival in Modern Astrology: A Preliminary History', available at *http://theafi.files.wordpress.com/2011/01/nick-campion_the-traditional-revival1.pdf* (accessed 9 May 2014); and in Kirk Little's, 'Defining the Moment: Geoffrey Cornelius and the Development of the Divinatory Approach', available at *http://www.astrozero.co.uk/articles/Defining.htm* (accessed 9 May 2014). An alternative view of the traditional approach is given by John Frawley in his article 'What is the tradition in astrology?', the Carter Memorial lecture, available at *http://www.johnfrawley.com/#!articles/c14j7* (accessed 9 May 2014).

page 204: **'John Frawley, who cites William Lilly as a major influence ...'** John Frawley's successful public predictions are discussed in Gary Phillipson's *Astrology in the Year Zero* (Flare Publications, 2000).

Index

Culpeper, Nicholas 40, 54–5, 148, 152
anti-establishment sentiments 106–7
democracy, prediction of 114, 115
solar eclipse, congregating for 109–10, 111–12, 117
speaking engagement at the Society of Astrologers 100

Daniel, Humphrey 101
The Dark Year (Lilly) 117, 118
De Judiciis Geniturarum (Cardano) 25, 129
Declaration of Indulgence 185–6
Dee, Dr John 73, 190–1
Delahay, Dr Richard 43
Digby, Sir Kenelm 191
Doctrine of Nativities (Gadbury) 133, 140, 150
Dryden, John 173, 192

East, Anne 136–8
eclipses 79–81
predictable and natural 111
solar *see* solar eclipse
Edlin, Richard 153, 162
elections 70, 72–3
Elizabeth I, Queen 16
England's Prophetical Merlin (Lilly) 24, 25, 46, 139, 150

equatorium 130
Evans, John 43–5, 62, 191

A Faire in Spittle Fields 123
Fairfax, Sir Thomas 30, 60–1, 63, 69, 77, 128
fanatics: seizure of 146–7
Farmer, Ralph 105
Fifth Monarchy 144
coming of 114–15, 115–16
The glorious rising of the Fifth Monarchy 115–16
Fiske, Nicholas 40, 45, 102
Forman, Simon 45, 61–2, 95, 191
Frawley, John 204–5
Frederick, King of Bohemia 62

Gadbury, John
appearance 131–2
apprenticeship in tailoring 131, 132
data collection 172, 173
experimental method 172, 176
grand vision for astrology 171–2
imprisonment 196
libelling Lilly 150–1
malicious insinuations about Lilly 141, 149, 150
patronage of Lilly 132
Pope-burning demonstration 195–6
prophetic side of astrology, disapproval of 176

radicalism 148
recalculation of astronomical tables 132
scorpion reference 149–50
sharing Lilly's study at Corner House 132, 133
star science, elite role of 174–5
Garraway's 153, 154
Gataker, Thomas 135–6
Gatehouse prison 143, 147
Gaule, John 123
Gaurico, Luca (*Tractatus astrologicus*) 129
Gell, Robert (*Government of the World by Angels*) 102
The glorious rising of the Fifth Monarchy 115–16
Goad, John 173
Government of the World by Angels (Gell) 102
Grand Remonstrance 4, 78
Great Fire of London 159–61, 160, 162–3
Gresham College 40, 41, 153
Gresham, Edward 150, 151
Gretton, Nicholas 148
Groby, Lord Grey of: meeting Lilly and Hugh Peter 82

Harflete, Henry 101, 114
Harmonicon Coeleste (Wing) 102
Hart, Alexander 42
Hartgill's tables 132

Reviews of *The Story of V*
by Catherine Blackledge

'A marvellous manifesto that points towards a new view of sexuality' —Jerome Burne, *Financial Times*

'A meticulous guide not only to the vagina, but to changing perceptions of womanhood' —*Observer*

'A persuasive and exhaustive study of the history, culture and reproductive power of female genitalia – the author is a phenomenal researcher and movingly enthusiastic about her special subject' —Joanne Briscoe, *Guardian*

'Her quest moves from the mythic to the scientific, presented in a lively, accessible style – an empowering and enlightening book' —Katie Donovan, *Irish Times*

'A serious and well-researched look at how attitudes and information have changed over the centuries ... This would be a great book to give to your man for his birthday. If you've got a girlfriend, well, read it together. It is completely fascinating' —Jeanette Winterson

'*The Story of V* reveals the ancient and newfound powers of the vagina. It is full of mystery and secrets and truth. If we only knew what we had under our skirts! Learn the story – read this book' —Eve Ensler, author, *The Vagina Monologues*

WATKINS

Sharing Wisdom Since
1893

The story of Watkins Publishing dates back to March 1893, when John M. Watkins, a scholar of esotericism, overheard his friend and teacher Madame Blavatsky lamenting the fact that there was nowhere in London to buy books on mysticism, occultism or metaphysics. At that moment Watkins was born, soon to become the home of many of the leading lights of spiritual literature, including Carl Jung, Rudolf Steiner, Alice Bailey and Chögyam Trungpa.

Today our passion for vigorous questioning is still resolute. With over 350 titles on our list, Watkins Publishing reflects the development of spiritual thinking and new science over the past 120 years. We remain at the cutting edge, committed to publishing books that change lives.

DISCOVER MORE ...

Read our blog

Watch and listen to
our authors in action

Sign up to
our mailing list

JOIN IN THE CONVERSATION

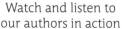

WatkinsPublishing   @watkinswisdom

WatkinsPublishingLtd   +watkinspublishing1893

Our books celebrate conscious, passionate, wise and happy living.
Be part of the community by visiting

www.watkinspublishing.com

DR CATHERINE BLACKLEDGE
is an author and journalist whose
career and interests span the
worlds of science and the occult.
Her first book, *The Story of V,* an
internationally acclaimed biography
of the vagina, has been translated into ten languages.
Born in 1968, she has a science degree and PhD and
has been a student of astrology for over a decade,
since studying the history of science and magic
fanned a fascination with the arcane art. She lives in
northwest England with her husband and daughter.